Glories Seen & Unseen

— *A Study of the Head Covering*

Warren Henderson

Glories Seen & Unseen (3rd edition)
By Warren Henderson
Copyright © 2007

Published by Warren Henderson
P.O. 416
Colfax, WI 54730

Cover Design by Jabe Nicholson Jr.
and John Nicholson

ISBN 978-0-9795387-2-8

ORDERING INFORMATION:

Gospel Folio Press	Scroll Publishing
1-800-952-2382	(717) 349-7033
www.gospelfolio.com	www.scrollpublishing.com
or various online retailers	

Printed in the United States of America

Table of Contents

3rd Edition

Since the original publication of Glories Seen &
Unseen in early 2002 and the subsequent edition
later that year, a number of questions and comments have been received by the author; the
overwhelming majority of these have been posi-
tive and constructive. For this reason, the book
has been revised again to include more questions
and answers material, and the text has been en-
riched with more devotional content.

Acknowledgements

The author cannot express his gratitude enough to
those who have aided this undertaking. A special
thanks to Mike Attwood and David Dunlap for
technical review, and to J.B. Nicholson Jr. and
John Nicholson for the cover design and layout. I
am grateful to Jane Biberstein, Karen Cyborski,
Gina Mulligan, David Lindstrom, and my beloved wife Brenda for proof reading assistance
and to Larry Sax for his Greek language counsel.
And most of all thanks and praise be unto my
Lord and Savior – Jesus Christ!

Introduction

Do you appreciate a brain-cramping mystery? Humanly speaking, the Old Testament is packed full of puzzling bits of divine expression – these are referred to as mysteries in the Bible. Formerly, in ancient days, the master plan of redeeming mankind was completely concealed in the mind of God. Why did God shroud His magnificent plan of salvation in secrecy? Paul explains why. The enemy would not have crucified the Lord Jesus if he had known that through His blood God would save repentant sinners (1 Cor. 2:8-9). Yet, even with the plan of redemption locked away safely in the recesses of divinity, glimpses of Calvary are seen throughout the Old Testament in the form of narrative, symbols, analogies, types, and names. After Christ ascended into heaven, God safely lifted the veil over these previously hidden truths through explanation in the New Testament epistles. Truly, the "New is in the Old contained, but the Old is by the New explained." God's teaching of the head covering follows this same mysterious pattern. The New Testament (1 Cor. 11) explains what has already been exemplified in the Old Testament.

Many Christians simply brush off the question of whether or not a woman should cover her head while she is praying or during meetings of the church. They consider the topic to be of low priority. What real significance does a head covering have in the 21st century anyway? On a relative scale of importance, the head covering certainly ranks lower than evangelism, holy living, Christology and many other central Christian teachings. To neglect these scriptural matters while arguing about the relevance

1

of this subject can only bring upon us the same "woe" Jesus pronounced upon the Pharisees in Matthew 23:23. "Weightier" doctrines of the Christian faith deserve a greater portion of our study time. But Jesus concluded His stinging reproof to the Pharisees by stating that they should not neglect the less significant teachings of God either. No portion of Scripture, however trivial in our own minds, ought to be neglected. It is all the word of God, and God proclaimed it for our benefit.

William Kelly, commenting on 1 Corinthians chapter 11, eloquently describes why this seemingly insignificant portion of Scripture manifests the awe of God:

> ...what a wonderful thing it is, and what power it shows, to be able to combine in the same epistle eternal things and the very smallest matter of personal decorum, the wearing of long hair or short, the use of a covering on the head or not! How truly it marks God and his word! Men would scorn to combine them both in the same epistle; it seems so petty and so incongruous. But it is the littleness of man which calls for big matters to make him important; but the smallest things of God have significance when they bear on the glory of Christ, as they always do.[1]

What importance did the apostle Paul bequeath to the matter of head coverings? Inspired by the Holy Spirit he penned 15 verses (1 Cor. 11:2-16), then immediately devoted the same space, 15 verses, to the subject of the Lord's Supper (1 Cor. 11:20-34). In one chapter, he corrects abuses in both these realms of Christian conduct. Consequently, we have three critical "glories" and three "symbols" which are fundamental to the Christian faith in this concise portion of Scripture. We conclude that these two topics of 1 Corinthians chapter 11 were serious issues and should not be diminished today by traditional or cultural arguments. There is no record of Paul writing on either of these two subjects again. Perhaps this is because the epistle was not only addressed to the saints at Corinth, but also to those who "in every place call upon the name of Jesus Christ" (1 Cor. 1:2). If you call upon the name of Christ, the contents of the whole letter (including chapter 11) are then applicable to you!

So, what does the Bible specifically teach about head covering? Should women wear a head covering today during church meetings or at other times? What were the headdress practices of the early Church? Is a woman's hair an acceptable covering for her? Was Paul's teaching only addressing converted prostitutes? These and many more questions will be addressed within the confines of this book.

Confusion over Biblical issues need not lead to controversy! Where there is a desire to learn from Scripture and an open heart to submit to revealed truth, God will bless with understanding. No child of God should stick their fingers in their ears and scurry from our Father's instruction. To do so invites the chastening hand of divine love upon us (Heb. 12:6). Instead, let anger give way to joy, and fear transition to faith, and for what we yet do not understand, let us have a spirit of reverence, awe, and humility – for vast are the mysteries that yet reside in the confines of God's mind (Rom. 11:33).

What is Symbolic Truth?

"If they have wings, why don't they use 'em?" bolstered a 17-year-old student during a Bible study on Spiritual Beings. She was perplexed. Why would God create spiritual creatures with multiple pairs of wings and then not allow them to use all their wings for flying? The Seraphim have six wings, but only use two for flying (Isa. 6). The Cherubim were given four wings, but only use two for the activity of flying (Ezek. 1). "But they are using their wings," I replied. "All of their wings are complying with God's intended purpose for each. Some are used for flying, and some for covering. These heavenly creatures are willfully covering themselves in the presence of God." After a moment of quandary the student retorted, "But why is it necessary for holy creatures to cover themselves in God's presence?" "Good question," I replied, then proceeded to explain to the class the case of "symbolic truth" that was before us. The bottom line: no other glory will compete with God's outshining awe. These exquisite creatures willfully conceal their own intrinsic glories with the very provision God had given them – their non-flying wings. Why did God take such care to create the Seraphim with six wings and the Cherubim with four wings? To ensure that all "competing glories" would be hidden and to provide a visible representation of divine order throughout the dominion of Almighty God.

The prophet Ezekiel informs us that Lucifer, literally "the light bearer," was a perfect and beautiful creature. He was a "covering" cherub, sheathed with precious stones and equipped inherently to worship God through music (Ezek. 28:11-16).

However, his prestigious position in creation and unique vantage point of God's preeminence led Lucifer to be dissatisfied with God's creation order. Lucifer no longer desired to cover himself. He would no longer conceal his personal glory in God's presence. His insubordination was energized by his pride to be "lifted up" and to be like the "Most High" (Isa. 14:14). Lucifer wanted the supremacy in heaven and led a rebellion against Almighty God, who responded by casting him off the Holy Mount and destining him to eternal judgment. Isaiah 42:8 reads, "I am the Lord: that is my name; and my glory will I not give to another, neither my praise to carved images." What competing glories will God tolerate in His presence? None.

What is symbolic truth? Simply stated, it is an act or object that epitomizes a spiritual fact. God knows that we are forgetful creatures, so He surrounds us with constant reminders of Himself, lest we forget His accomplishments. The book of Deuteronomy, which means "second law," was given by God for the purpose of reminding the Jews not to forget His commandments. God even wrote His commandments on two stones for a visible reminder of His law. Circumcision was a reminder to every Jew that they were God's chosen people and under a divine covenant. The temple and the tabernacle were reminders that God dwelled among his people; however, the many coverings used in these structures also gave testimony to God's holy and unapproachable existence. The Passover Feast was instituted to remind the Jews of God's deliverance from Egypt. Joshua was commanded to take 12 stones from a dry Jordan River bed and erect an historical monument attesting to the miracle God had performed.

The New Testament also uses "symbolic truth" for stimulating our memory and revealing God's fuller meaning of Scripture. In fact, an angel explained to John that the "Revelation of Jesus Christ" would be shown to him through symbols (Rev. 1:1). Before one can understand the book of Revelation, one must first understand the literal use of these symbols. One would be baffled over the description of the Lord Jesus as having seven horns, if the description were not understood to be symbolic. A "horn" represents "power," and the number "seven" conveys "perfection;" thus, the Lord is all-powerful. Only by understanding symbolic truth may the vastness of the conveyed message be grasped. The New Testament also contains visible tokens to aid our minds in remembering the precious spiritual truths. Examples of these tokens would include the Lord's Supper, believer's (water) baptism, and the head covering.

To have a broad appreciation for New Testament teaching on the head covering, one must first understand the symbolic meaning of "coverings." Previously, it was shown that spiritual beings have a means of covering their own intrinsic glory in God's presence. Their non-flying wings serve in two capacities – to "conceal" their own glory and to "reveal" God's glory and order. Indeed, Biblical coverings enable two contrasting realities to exist together in harmony. Something that should be "concealed" is covered, and something that should not be veiled is "revealed."

After the fall of man, Adam and Eve covered themselves with fig leaves. This covering, although it covered their nakedness, did not represent the holiness of God. The fig leaves represented a bloodless system of human works rather than redemption through an innocent substitutional sacrifice – it did not picture Christ's future work at Calvary. God killed innocent animals, took their skins, and fashioned clothes for Adam and the woman. The death of these animals typified the future substitutional sacrifice of God's Son – the Lord Jesus. God would have no competing "systems" to His plan of redemption and gave coverings to represent that fact. The animal skins "concealed" man's shame (a consequence of sin) and "revealed" God's righteous solution to forgive man's sin.

Rebekah took a veil and covered herself when she understood Isaac (her espoused husband) was approaching her from the field (Gen. 24:64-65). Her veil showed practical submission to Isaac. By concealing her own head, she was visibly proclaiming that she was relinquishing self-rule and acknowledging

7

Isaac's authority over her. This action was in accordance with her parents' authority concerning the marriage covenant also. Thus, Rebekah was signifying God's family order through the veil. Her action was not, strictly speaking, an issue of modesty, for her head had been uncovered in the presence of the men escorting her back from Mesopotamia.

The Tabernacle was full of coverings. The tent of meeting consisted of four layers of coverings (woven linen with cherubim embroidered in blue, goat's hair, ram's skin and badger's skin). Veils of fine woven linen hung between the most holy place and the holy place and between the holy place and the courtyard. Even a 7.5 foot white linen curtain hung upon 56 pillars about the courtyard to prevent anyone from looking in. Each veil declared God's holiness and man's sinfulness. Man could not casually venture into His presence and survive. Thus, God's holiness was "concealed" from man's direct eyesight lest he should die, but the coverings "revealed" a solution called atonement. Inside the veil, where God dwelt, sins were being covered by the blood of animals. This atonement allowed God to dwell among his people, but in a concealed fashion.

Korah's rebellion, as recorded in Numbers chapter 16, is another example of the importance of coverings. As a Kohathite, Korah was tasked with bearing the "covered" tabernacle furnishings from one desert campsite to another. The Kohathites were forbidden to directly gaze upon the holy furnishings; however, they were allowed to enter the tabernacle and carry the furnishings after Aaron and his sons had covered them. What an honor Korah had! However, he was lifted up with pride and rebelled against his God-appointed role. He even sought to be the high priest. Korah committed the same sin as Lucifer – he wanted the leadership position and the glory that came with it. There was no desire to adhere to God's order. As God had cast Lucifer off the holy mount and destined him to the Lake of Fire, He now caused the ground to open up and swallow Korah and his family alive. God is competent in recompensing rebels with justice. He severely judged those who did not want to follow His prescribed order. Why did Korah and Lucifer rebel against their role of covering? Because it represented God-ordained order.

Even the flesh of the Lord Jesus was called a veil (Heb. 10:20). His flesh "concealed" His inherent divine glory, but still "revealed" the righteous character of God through His humanity. Certainly, this reality provides the platform for Paul's teaching on the head covering in 1 Corinthians 11. When the local church gathers into the presence of God, there is to be a glory "revealed" and glories "concealed" by the coverings. God's glory is seen in the uncovered heads of men, while man's glory – the woman, and the woman's glory – her hair are to be concealed by a covering.

We conclude that God is pleased when created beings submit to His created order. This submission is shown in practice and in symbolism through the use of coverings. God is glorified in heaven when created beings freely choose to conceal their own intrinsic glory. In the same way, God is glorified when, through the use of coverings, His divine order is seen in the local church. Thus, the local church meetings are to mimic the same scene of humility that exists at all times before the throne of the universe. This symbolic practice of covering ensures that only the glory of Almighty God is seen and all other competing glories remain unseen. Proper covering gives the visible evidence of order in the heavenly realms as well as in the assemblies of God's people on earth. Divine order is fundamental and central to the proper functioning of any local church, and it should thus be expressed symbolically in the church's public gatherings through the head covering.

What is the importance of practicing symbolic truth in the church today? It is indeed as important today as in the day these symbols were given by God for our benefit. John Chrysostom, a fourth century preacher from Antioch, graphically describes the error of neglecting symbolic truth:

For perhaps some one might here have doubt also, questioning with himself, what sort of a crime it was for the woman to be uncovered, or the man covered? What sort of crime it is, learn now from hence. Symbols many and diverse have been given both to man and woman; to him of rule, to her of subjection: and among them this also, that she should be covered, while he hath his head bare. If now these be symbols you see that both err when they disturb the proper order, and transgress the disposition of God, and their own proper limits, both the man falling into the woman's inferiority, and the woman rising up against the man by her outward habiliments.... When therefore thou overturnest these boundaries, see how great injuries ensue. And tell me not this, that the error is but small. For first, it is great even of itself: being as it is disobedience. Next, though it were small, it became great because of the greatness of the things whereof it is a sign. However, that it is a great matter, is evident from its ministering so effectually to good order among mankind, the governor and the governed being regularly kept in their several places by it. So that he who transgresseth disturbs all things, and betrays the gifts of God, and casts to the ground the honor bestowed on him from above; not however the man only, but also the woman. For to her also it is the greatest of honors to preserve her own rank; as indeed of disgraces, the behavior of a rebel.[1]

Old Testament Headdress Practices

The Old Testament records over four millennia of human history. The first mention of a head covering practice among women occurs in Genesis chapter 24, roughly halfway through the Old Testament's chronology of human affairs. We learn that Rebekah was accustomed to wearing a veil in public. Although it is likely that women were veiled prior to this account, it cannot be biblically asserted.

Tamar is the next example of a woman veiling herself in the Bible. Her husband had died, and the custom was for the widow to illustrate mourning by wearing widow's clothing. She was waiting for her dead husband's younger brother to reach marrying age so that she could be married again and bear children. However, after knowing that Judah, her father-in-law, had deceived her, she determined to change her clothing. In order to deceive Judah and conceive children in the name of her dead husband, she wore the worship attire of a Canaanite goddess, thus identifying herself as a Canaanite prostitute (Gen. 38:15). The plan worked, and she conceived twins, one of whom is in the genealogy of Christ. Besides the fact that women were covered in public, Tamar's action also demonstrates that it was not always a universal custom for prostitutes to uncover their heads.

Another reference to women covering themselves is found in Numbers 5:18. We are informed that a priest removed a woman's veil after sitting her before the Lord and invoking the "jealousy test." Other references to women veiling include Ruth

3:15 (her veil was most likely a cloak), Isaiah 3:20, 23; and Song of Solomon 5:7.

What about the Jewish men? Did they wear head coverings? Scripture commanded that a "miter" be worn by the high priest while ministering in the tabernacle (Ex. 28:4). Upon the forefront of this miter the high priest had to also wear the "golden plate, the holy crown" (Lev. 8:9). While working in the tabernacle this gold crown upon the high priest's head represented the glory of God in lieu of his uncovered head. Not just in the priest's headdress, but throughout the entire Jewish economy of worship the Lord intricately uses symbols to represent His own divine glory and also human depravity.

Jewish men might cover their heads in response to shame, disgrace, and mourning. In 1 Samuel 4:12, the man bearing the news of the loss of the ark of covenant had covered his head with dirt. The man who brought David news of Saul's death also covered his head with earth (2 Sam. 1:2). David responded to the news of Absalom's rebellion by fleeing Jerusalem with his head literally covered. All the men that were with David also covered their heads (2 Sam. 15:30), and when Hushai arrived to meet David (2 Sam. 15:32), he likewise had earth upon his head. The nobles of Judah covered their heads in response to the terrible drought conditions that threatened their lives (Jer. 14:3-4). In Isaiah 37:1-3, King Hezekiah covered himself with sackcloth, probably including his head, in response to blasphemy by Rabshakeh. Hezekiah said it was a day of rebuke and disgrace. After Haman honored his enemy, Mordecai, by leading him through streets on the royal steed, he returned home with his head covered (Est. 6:12). Although Haman was not a Jew, his actions displayed the consistency of men in the Old Testament to cover their heads during a time of shame, mourning, or disgrace. However, Jewish men of the Bible normally did not cover their heads in public.

But why do Jewish men wear a head covering today? Perhaps some of the Jews had begun following the tradition of the

Greeks in wearing a beanie-type head covering known as a "ki-pa" or "yarmulke." Perhaps, the Greeks who wore hats during sporting events influenced Jewish men (2 Maccabees 4:9-13). Jewish authorities admit there is no Biblical basis allowing or commanding men to wear a head covering as they do today.

Let Church History Speak

When evaluating the profitability of a particular behavior or custom, it is normally beneficial to peer into history for its relevance. Certainly, a review of church history is helpful in ascertaining how our church forefathers understood 1 Corinthians chapter 11 down through the church age. Although we don't like to admit it, we often flavor "the application of Scripture" by our own social dogmas and experiences. It is quite possible to be agreed with another on "the meaning" of Scripture, but disagreed on "the application." The Lord's Supper is a good example. Most evangelical Christians would be agreed on the symbolic meaning of this remembrance meeting, but not on how it should be conducted. By reviewing church history, we tap into a variety of social vantage points and lessen the threat of obscuring the plain meaning of Scripture by cultural variations.

What did our church forefathers teach concerning the head covering? Is there a consistent pattern of application? Below are three dozen historical inferences and quotes from theologians and scholars bridging the gap between the apostolic age and the present time. Let it not be said that these excerpts are narrow, for these brethren come from the widest variation of Christian backgrounds, churches, denominations, and theological studies. The inferred dates, which follow the name of the writer, are reflective of either the author's life span or the year the associated reference was published.

Historical Writings during the Church Age:

Hermas (1st or 2nd Century AD)

A virgin meets me, adorned as if she were proceeding from the bridal chamber ... her head was covered by a hood.[1]

Irenaeus (130-200 AD)

Irenaeus translates 1 Corinthians 11:10 as follows: "A woman ought to have a veil [kalumma] upon her head, because of the angels."[2]

Clement of Alexandria/Titus Flavius Clement (150-215 AD)

A contemporary of Tertullian, he saw a spiritual connection between devotion to Christ and a woman's wearing of a veil. In his book, *The Instructor*, Clement writes, "Women and men are to go to the assembly decently attired, possessing unfeigned love, pure in body, pure in heart, fit to pray to God. Let the women observe further. Let her be entirely covered, unless she be at home. And she will never fall, who unites devotion and modesty with her veil. For this is the wish of the Word, since it is becoming for her to pray veiled."[3]

Clement also understands the words in 1 Corinthians 11:5 to refer to a veil of fabric and not to a woman's hair. "And she will never fall, who puts before her eyes modesty, and her shawl; nor will she invite another to fall into sin by uncovering her face. For this is the wish of the Word, since it is becoming for her to pray veiled" [1 Corinthians 11:5]. "It has also been commanded that the head should be veiled and the face covered. For it is a wicked thing for beauty to be a snare to men."[4]

Tertullian (160-230 AD)

Tertullian was a fiery Christian writer from Carthage, North Africa. He believed that the covering for women was not bound by culture or time, but that it was a timeless biblical principle. Writing about 160 years after Paul's letter to Corinth, he states,

"For throughout Greece, and in certain of its barbaric provinces, the majority of churches keep their women covered. So let no one ascribe this custom merely to the Gentile customs of the Greeks and barbarians. The Corinthians themselves understood him (the Apostle Paul) to speak in this manner. For to this very day the Corinthians veil their virgins. So, on both sides of the matter, the apostle has written with sufficient clarity, in fact he says quite succinctly, 'every woman.' What does 'every' mean if it doesn't mean every class, every order, every condition, and every age."[5]

Tertullian, like most of his contemporaries, had a deep concern for modesty. He also stressed veiled heads for modesty's sake, but he seems to apply the principle with a severity not taught in the New Testament. He also expressed a concern that the veiling be worn consistently out of the assembly as well as in it. "Identity (sameness) of nature abroad as at home, identity (sameness) of custom in the presence of men as of the Lord, consists in identity (sameness) of liberty. To what purpose, then, do they thrust their glory out of sight abroad, but expose it in the church? I demand a reason. Is it to please the brethren, or God Himself …? What cannot appear to be done for God's sake (because God wills not that it be done in such a way) is done for the sake of men – a thing, of course, primarily lawful, as betraying a lust for glory."[6]

Hippolytus (170-236 AD)

Hippolytus was a leading elder in the Church of Rome near the beginning of the third century. "And let all the women have their heads covered with an opaque cloth, not with a veil of thin linen, for this is not a true covering." The worship practices of the early church are described by Hippolytus "Canon Seventeenth. Of virgins, that they should cover their faces and their heads."[7]

John Chrysostom (340-407 AD)

Chrysostom was the great preacher of Antioch. Chrysostom identifies the problem Paul addresses in 1 Corinthians 11:2-16 as "Their women used to pray and prophesy unveiled and with their head bare." Chrysostom, commenting on verse 5, taught that a woman needed a separate head covering other than her long hair:

> 'And if it be given her for a covering,' say you, 'wherefore need she add another covering?' That not nature only, but also her own will may have part in her acknowledgment of subjection. For that thou oughtest to be covered nature herself by anticipation enacted a law. Add now, I pray, thine own part also, that thou mayest not seem to subvert the very laws of nature; a proof of most insolent rashness, to buffet not only with us, but with nature also.

> For a man indeed ought not to have his head veiled, forasmuch as he is the image and glory of God (1 Cor. 11:7). This again is another cause [why the woman should be covered]. 'Not only,' so he speaks, 'because he hath Christ to be His Head ought he not to cover the head, but because also he rules over the woman.' For the ruler when he comes before the king ought to have the symbol of his rule. As therefore no ruler without military girdle and cloak, would venture to appear before him that hath the diadem: so neither do thou without the symbols of thy rule, (one of which is the not being covered,) pray before God, lest thou insult both thyself and Him that hath honored thee. And the same thing likewise one may say regarding the woman. For to her also is it a reproach, the not having the symbols of her subjection. 'But the woman is the glory of the man'.

> ... It follows that being covered is a mark of subjection and authority. For it induces her to look down and be ashamed and preserve entire her proper virtue. For the virtue and honor of the governed is to abide in his obedience.[8]

The Constitutions of the Holy Apostles (250-325 AD)
Finally, let me suggest that there are fragments of the apostle's (Paul) instructions everywhere scattered throughout his epistles, such as the minute canon concerning the veiling of women in acts of worship, insisting upon it with a length of argument which in one of the apostolic fathers would be considered childish. He also insisted that his tradition is from the Lord.[9]

Apostolic Constitutions (390 AD)
When you are in the streets, cover your head. For by such a covering, you will avoid being viewed by idle persons....[10]

Jerome (345-429 AD)
It is usual in the monasteries of Egypt and Syria for virgins and widows who have vowed themselves to God and have renounced the world and have trodden under foot its pleasures, to ask the mothers of their communities to cut their hair; not that afterwards they go about with heads uncovered in defiance of the apostles command.[11]

Augustine (354-430 AD)
Writing to his friend, Possidius, an elder in a local church, Augustine details the relationship of spiritual headship in the home and spiritual headship in the church: "Those who belong to this world have also to consider how they may please their wives if they be husbands, their husbands if they be wives, with this limitation, that it is not becoming for women to uncover their hair, since the apostle commands women to keep their heads covered."[12]

Commenting on 1 Cor. 11:7, "... especially when the Apostle says that the man is the image of God, and on that account, removes the covering from his head, which he warns the woman to use, speaking thus...." "'Every man praying or prophesying with veiled head shameth his head;' and, 'A man ought not to veil his head, forsomuch as he is the image and glory of God.'"

Now if it is true of a man that he is not to veil his head, then the opposite is true of a woman, that she is to veil her head. "We ought not therefore so to understand that made in the image of the Supreme Trinity, that is, in the image of God, as that same image should be understood to be in three human beings; especially when the apostle says that the man is the image of God, and on that account removes the covering from his head, which he warns the woman to use, speaking thus: 'For a man indeed ought not to cover his head, forasmuch as he is the image and glory of God; but the woman is the glory of the man.'" Augustine insisted that women keep their hair covered in public. "It is not becoming even in married women to uncover their hair, since the apostle commands the women to keep their heads covered.... For she is instructed for this very reason to cover her head, which he is forbidden to do because he is the image of God."[13]

8th Century Summary (English Culture)

It is likely that headgear for women was becoming more common by the seventh century. It seems that Christian morality (based on St Paul's edicts) was influential in this respect. By the eighth century it seems that head coverings were worn by all women. It seems that a close fitting cap was worn by most women (perhaps similar to the slightly later caps from York and Dublin), which sometimes left the hair at the forehead and temples visible.[14]

11th and 12th Century Summary

Modern hat designer Madeleine Ginsburg explains how the hat evolved through the centuries. Apparently, hoods were worn for warmth and everyday use, and a hat with a high crown and wide brim was worn for traveling through about the 11th century. Ginsburg writes, "The shape of the cap and hood are so dictated by function there has been, on a basic level, little change in a thousand years ... some shapes are still with us."[15] Women apparently started to adorn themselves with veils at about this time.

In the 11th and 12th century it is very unusual to see a man wearing a hat, though the women, unless they are very young or representing some virtue, inevitably have some sort of headdress on...while most women wore something that was more or less a derivative of a veil.[16]

... I have looked at dozens and hundreds of illuminations, pictures and medieval artifacts that portray people in the civilian dress of various periods and my observation is that you can't generalize. All through the Early Christian, Migration and Carolingian Eras you don't see many people with hats on, although you see an occasional crown, the women are inevitably veiled and many of the soldiers are wearing helmets.[17]

John Knox (1505-1572 AD)

First, I say, the woman in her greatest perfection was made to serve and obey man, not to rule and command him. As saint Paule doth reason in these wordes: 'Man is not of the woman, but the woman of the man. ... therfore oght [ought] the woman to have a power upon her head,' (that is, a coverture in sign of subjection).[18]

John Calvin (1509-1564 AD)

Calvin preached three sermons from 1 Corinthians 11:2-16 from which the following excerpts are taken.

So if women are thus permitted to have their heads uncovered and to show their hair, they will eventually be allowed to expose their entire breasts, and they will come to make their exhibitions as if it were a tavern show; they will become so brazen that modesty and shame will be no more; in short they will forget the duty of nature.... So, when it is permissible for the women to uncover their heads, one will say, 'Well, what harm in uncovering the stomach also?' And then after that one will plead [for] something else: 'Now if the women go bareheaded, why not also [bare] this and [bare] that?' Then the men, for their part, will break loose too. In short, there will be no decency left, unless people contain themselves and respect what is proper and fitting, so as not to go headlong overboard.

Hence we infer that the woman has her hair given her for a covering. Should any one now object, that her hair is enough, as being a natural covering, Paul says that it is not, for it is such a covering as requires another thing to be made use of for covering it. And hence a conjecture is drawn, with some appearance of probability – that women who had beautiful hair were accustomed to uncover their heads for the purpose of showing off their beauty. It is not, therefore, without good reason that Paul, as a remedy for this vice, sets before them the opposite idea – that they be regarded as remarkable for unseemliness, rather than for what is an incentive to lust.[19]

George Gillespie (1613-1648 AD)

Gillespie, speaking concerning the church meetings in his own Westminster Assembly:

But where find we that women who were prophetesses, and immediately inspired, were allowed to deliver their prophecy in the church? I suppose he had a respect to 1 Cor. xi:5, "But every woman that prayeth or prophesieth with her head uncovered, dishonoreth her head," which is meant of the public assembly, for the Apostle is speaking of covering or uncovering the head in the church…. So that the Geneva annotation upon ver. 5, gives a good sense of that text, "That women which show themselves in public and ecclesiastical assemblies, without the sign and token of their subjection, that is to say, uncovered, shame themselves."[20]

Matthew Henry (1662-1714 AD)

It was the common usage of the churches for women to appear in public assemblies, and join in public worship veiled; and it was manifestly decent that they should do so. Those must be very contentious indeed who would quarrel with this or lay it aside.[21]

John Wesley (1703-1791 AD)

For a man indeed ought not to veil his head because he is the image and glory of God in the dominion he bears over the creation, representing the supreme dominion of God, which is his glory. But the woman is a matter of glory to the man, who has a becoming dominion over her. Therefore she ought not to appear except with her head veiled as a tacit acknowledgment of it.[22]

Henry Alford (1810-1871 AD)

[1 Corinthians 11] 2-16. The law of subjection of the woman to the man (2-12), and natural decency itself (13-16), teach that women should be veiled in public religious assemblies.[23]

Frederick Godet (1812-1900 AD)

The phrase [in 1 Corinthians 11:4], 'having down from the head,' that is to say, wearing a kerchief in the form of a veil coming down from the head over the shoulders. And since the woman does not naturally belong to public life, if it happen that in the spiritual domain she has to exercise a function which brings her into prominence, she ought to strive the more to put herself out of view by covering herself with the veil, which declares the dependence in which she remains relatively to her husband.[24]

19th Century Summary (Western Culture)

Women in the 19th century kept their heads modestly covered most of the time. They wore "day caps" of fine linen or cotton, with ruffles around the face, and chin ties. These were even worn under the cape hood, or under the summer straw bonnet or winter quilted bonnet. Ladies of fashion wore elaborately decorated bonnets when they left home: flowers, feathers, lace, ribbons, ruchings and ruffles abounded.

A. R. Fausset (1821-1910 AD)

… in putting away the veil, she puts away the badge of her subjection to man (which is her true 'honor'), and of her connection with Christ, man's Head. Moreover, the head covering was the emblem of maiden modesty before man (Gen. 24:65), and chastity (Gen. 20:16). By it unlawful excitement in assemblies is avoided, women not attracting attention. Scripture sanctions not the emancipation of woman from subjection: modesty is her true ornament.

"Christ" (1 Cor. 11:3), but literally, as "his head" is used in the beginning of the verse. *He dishonoreth his head* (the principal part of the body) by wearing a covering or veil, which is a mark of subjection, and which makes him look downwards instead of upwards to his Spiritual Head, Christ, to whom alone he owes subjection. Why, then, ought not man to wear the covering in token of his subjection to Christ, as the woman wears it in token of her subjection to man? "Because Christ is not seen: the man is seen; so the covering of him who is under Christ is not seen; of her who is under the man, is seen."[25]

M. R. Vincent (1886 AD)

The headdress of Greek women consisted of nets, hair-bags, or kerchiefs, sometimes covering the whole head. A shawl which enveloped the body was also often thrown over the head, especially at marriages or funerals. This costume the Corinthian women had disused in the Christian assemblies, perhaps as an assertion of the abolition of sexual distinctions, and the spiritual equality of the woman with the man in the presence of Christ. This custom was discountenanced by Paul as striking at the divinely ordained subjection of the woman to the man.[26]

G. G. Findlay (late 19th Century)

For a woman to discard the veil means to cast off masculine authority, which is a fixed part of the Divine order, like man's subordination to Christ (3 f.).[27]

Joseph Beet (late 19th and early 20th Century)

Unveiled: without the peplum or shawl, which Greek women wore usually on their shoulders, but in public over their heads. Now when men stand uncovered before God, and women covered, they accept formally and visibly by their own action this distinction of sex and the position in reference to the other sex which God has given.[28]

C. C. Walker (1900 AD)

Paul's direction was that women should be covered in the assemblies. The size of the assembly or the location of it does not alter the principle. There should be no contention over the matter. Paul cut it short authoritatively in his day: "If any man seem to be contentious, we have no such custom, neither the churches of God." Doubtless in very small meetings in private houses it seems strange for a sister to cover her head in her own house; but we remember that they broke bread from house to house in apostolic times, and we cannot suppose that the example of the Corinthian women would be tolerated because of the smallness of an assembly. Discerning sisters will gladly submit to the apostolic ruling.[29]

Watchman Nee (1903-1972)

The meaning of head covering is: I submit myself to God's government: I accept God's appointed position: I dare not nullify His government by the grace I have received; I do not even dare to think about it; on the contrary, I accept God's government. As Christ accepts God as His head, so should every man accept Christ as his head. Likewise, woman should representatively accept man as her head. In covering the head, the woman signifies that she is not head, that she is as if she has no head – for it is covered.... God calls upon the sisters to show this arrangement. It is through the sisters that God's governmental system is to be displayed. It is the sisters who are responsible to have the sign of obedience on their heads. God specifically requires women to have their head covered when praying or prophesying. Why? Because they ought to know God's government when they come before Him. In going before God to pray for people or in going before people to prophesy for God, whether in praying or in prophesying, whether in that which goes to God or in that which comes from God, in whatever is related to God, head covering is demanded. The purpose is to manifest the government of God....

Someday the whole world will know that Christ is the head of all men, for this is God's governmental decision. Today this is only known in the church; the world has no knowledge of it.... Likewise, God's appointment of man as head of woman is also known only in the church today. Do you get the point? Today the church alone knows that Christ is the head of man and that man is the head of woman.[30]

A. T. Robertson (1931 AD)

Commenting on 1 Corinthians 11:4 ("having his head covered"), he points out:

Literally, having a veil (*kalumma* understood) down from the head." Paul declares in 1 Corinthians 11:6, "Let her be veiled (*Katakaluptestho*).... Let her cover up herself with the veil (down, kata, the Greek says, the veil hanging down from the head).[31]

William Barclay (1954 AD)

Former Professor of Divinity and Bible Criticism at the University of Glasgow writes:

The problem was whether or not in the Christian Church a woman had the right to take part in the service unveiled. Paul's answer was bluntly this the veil is always a sign of subjection; it is worn by an inferior in the presence of a superior; now woman is inferior to man, in the sense that man is head of the household; therefore it is wrong for a man to appear at public worship veiled and it is equally wrong for a woman to appear unveiled.[32]

John Murray (1898-1975 AD)

On the matter of women being veiled Murray of Westminster Theological Seminary writes:

Since Paul appeals to the order of creation (Vss. 3b, vss 7ff), it is totally indefensible to suppose that what is in view and enjoined had only local or temporary relevance. The ordinance of creation is universally and perpetually applicable, as also are the implications for conduct arising there-from.

I am convinced that a head covering is definitely in view forbidden for the man (Vss 4 & 7) and enjoined for the woman (Vss 5, 6, 15). In the case of the woman the covering is not simply her long hair. This supposition would make nonsense of verse 6. For the thought there is, that if she does not have a covering she might as well be shorn or shaven, a supposition without any force whatever if the hair covering is deemed sufficient.[33]

J. Vernon McGee (1904-1990 AD)
Apparently some of the women in the church at Corinth were saying, "All things are lawful for me, therefore, I won't cover my head." Paul says this should not be done because the veil is a mark of subjection.[34]

Charles Caldwell Ryrie (1958)
Charles Ryrie, former professor at Dallas Theological Seminary explains a woman's role in worship:

A woman must have her head covered at worship, since that is the proper way for her to recognize the divine order of creation. ... If angels desire to look into things pertaining to salvation, then they should see as they look at veiled women in the assembly of Christians the voluntary submission of a woman to her head. Thus the early church (for this was the custom of the churches generally) while offering religious equality in spiritual privilege insisted on showing in public worship the principle of subordination of women by their being veiled.[35]

Albrect Oepke (1965 AD)

The veiling of women is a custom in Israel. A disgraced woman comes veiled to judgment (katakekalummene, Sus. 32). Yet one may suspect that a woman muffled up (kateka-lupsato to prosopon) and lurking by the wayside is a harlot (Gen. 38:15). This opens the way for an understanding of the relevant NT passage. The veiling of women in the NT and the contemporary world.[36]

Bruce Waltke (1978 AD)

Dr. Bruce Waltke, professor of the Old Testament at Regent College in Vancouver, BC writes:

If the church would include 1 Corinthians 11:2-16 in their readings at the Lord's Supper, they would be guarded against some extreme positions and theological errors. Unfortunately this has not been the case, and as a result many believers within the church are abandoning Paul's clear teaching on the subject.[37]

Although Paul does not use the word veil [kalumma GLP], it seems reasonable to suppose that he has this article of apparel in view.... To appear at the public assembly, then, with inappropriate headdress would disgrace one's head. A woman in an assembly of believers should cover her head as a symbol of her submission to the absolute will of God who ordered His Universe according to His own good pleasure. The symbol must be present or the reality and its truth may be lost. Thus the face with which God chose to reveal Himself to the world is one that the world desperately needs to see, namely, a man who displays the image and glory of God through Christ, and a woman who, though equal to man, submits to him. It would be well for Christian women to wear head coverings at church meetings as a symbol of an abiding theological truth.[38]

Noel Weeks (1988 AD)

There is something ludicrous about being the head or authority while one at the same time hides one's physical head. It follows therefore that praying and prophesying are authoritative functions which call for an unveiled head, unshrouded head. Hence any woman engaging in those activities must also be bare-headed. Consequently Paul turns to what such unveiling must mean for the woman. In contrast to the man, when she prays or prophesies, the unveiling of her head must be dishonorable to her. What does it mean for a woman to be bareheaded? As Paul says, it is equivalent to being shaved or having her hair shorn off. That of course is dishonouring for a woman. Hence she should not uncover her head.[39]

Robert D. Culver (1989 AD)

God distinguishes sharply between the sexes as to appearance and activity in formal Christian assemblies. A man's hair is to be short and his head uncovered by hat or shawl, while a woman's hair is to be uncut and, in visible recognition of submission to God's order, she is to wear an additional head covering in order to veil, not her face, but head.[40]

John Phillips (2002)

Here Paul, writing under the direct inspiration of the Holy Spirit, states that for a woman to pray or prophesy with her head uncovered means that she dishonors her head (the man) and that is the same, in God's sight, as though she were "shaven." If she disregards the covering, which is the symbol of her position, she may as well discard the natural covering God has given her (her hair) as well....

The word here for uncovered is *akatakalyptos*. It stems from *kalypto*, which means "to veil," to which is added the preposition *kata* (down). The reference is not to some token, such as a doily, but to a veil, a proper covering.[41]

Other Church leaders from the past and theologians of the present not quoted above also understood Paul's teaching on the head covering.

Men such as Martin Luther, David Dickson, Menno Simons, Albert Barnes, Adams Clarke, John Darby, William Kelly, C. H. Mackintosh, Ulrich Zwingli, John Lightfoot, Robert Lewis Dabney, M. R. Vincent, Thomas Charles Edwards, F. W. Grosheide, H. A. Ironside, Robert H. Gundry, Gordon Fee, George E. Meisinger, Thomas R. Schreiner, R. C. Sproul, William MacDonald, Dr. H. Wayne House, David Lowery, R. C. H. Lenski, and Charles Hodge. Even presently, if one would venture to the Internet, he or she would learn that a host of contemporary writers are still proclaiming the truth of the head covering via hundreds of websites.

A Message from Church Art

Ancient church art, as preserved in the Roman catacombs, depicts praying women as wearing the *palla,* a veil or scarf on the head, which hung down over her shoulders. The Roman catacombs were extensive underground cemeteries connected by numerous narrow tunnels beneath the city. These catacombs, sometimes six levels deep provided a safe haven for the church from brutal Roman persecution. The catacombs were dark, cold and damp with the stench of rotting flesh in the air. Yet the rock walls of the catacombs became the parchments for joyous Christian expression through artistic etchings and sculptures. See catacomb artwork depicting women veiled in Appendix A.

M. R. Vincent comments "In the sculptures of the catacombs the women have close-fitting head-dress, while the men have the hair short."[42] Also preserved is a Tenth Century AD drawing of a worshipping group of Christians: the men's heads are uncovered, and the women's heads are covered with veils. And finally, Rembrandt's beautiful painting "Preacher Anslo Giving Comfort to Women" shows the women's heads covered with a gauze veil.

Concerning the Roman Catholic Church

Bruce Waltke clearly defines the Roman Catholic teaching for the head covering:

Although Paul does not use the word veil [kalumma GLP], it seems reasonable to suppose that he has this article of apparel in view. … To appear at the public assembly, then, with inappropriate headdress would disgrace one's head.[43]

Before the revision in 1983, Canon law had stated that women must cover their heads "especially when they approach the holy table" (can.1262.2). But in order to reduce such a growing collection of books, the new version of Canon law was subjected to concise changes. In the process, mention of head coverings was omitted.

The second Vatican Council (1962-1965) was the pivotal point in history when many Roman Catholic women discontinued covering themselves during church meetings. Annibale Bugnini, then secretary of the Vatican Congregation for Divine Worship, in response to a question on the head covering, informed an anxious group of reporters that the Bishops were considering other issues, and that women's veils were not on the agenda. The following day, the international press proclaimed to the world that Catholic women no longer had to wear their veils in church services. Although a misquoted Bugnini later tried to correct the wrong, the media never retracted the error. Unfortunately, the pressure of fanatical feminist groups and the confusion about the church's position caused many women to stop wearing a veil during services.

Concerning the Orthodox Church

Orthodox women, according to the words of the holy Apostle Paul, go to God's church with covered heads. For nearly two thousand years now, this custom has been kept by faithful women and has been handed down from generation to generation. It is a custom not only of the local churches, but also of the Universal Church, and, therefore – whether we be in a Greek, in a Serbian or Russian church – the women in the church have their heads covered.[44]

31

From the editor of The Russian Orthodox publication Parish Life:

> From time immemorial, in all Orthodox countries believers were careful – not only by their conduct, but also by their dress – not to offend the holiness of the church. The church is a special place – heaven on earth. We must leave outside the walls of the church all the vanity and the secular principles of this world "that lies in sin," according to the expression of the Evangelist John the Theologian. We come to church to pray, and it is necessary to offer prayer in the modest attire of one "poor in spirit" and "meek in heart." Ladies! Cover your heads during prayer in church! Do not come to church in bright and seductive clothing![45]

Summary of the Head Covering Practice throughout Church History

What conclusions can be drawn from the testimonies of these church theologians, scholars and historians?

1. Historical research indicates that 1 Corinthians chapter 11 has generally been, until recent days, interpreted and understood to exhort women to cover their heads and men to uncover their heads during meetings of the church and/or during the spiritual exercise of prayer and teaching.

2. Though the motive for teaching the woman's head covering (modesty, submission, status of virginity, concealing human glories, necessity to teach, etc.) and the type of head covering worn varied throughout the church age, the practice itself did not decline until the early 20th century.

3. During the far majority of the church age, women covered their heads in public as well. This is especially true during the Middle Ages and the Puritan era.

Early church history indicates that the woman's head covering was the norm in Antioch, Rome, and Africa. The apostle Thomas took the gospel to India and also taught the converts to Christ the importance of the head covering practice, which the Christian women have continued to obey even unto this day. Presently, the head covering practice is occurring in many African, Asian, and Eastern European Christian churches. The author can personally attest to meeting Chinese Christians in the underground church who are following the head covering teaching. In many of these churches, there has been no Western contact or explanation on this subject ever, yet these dear sisters have strong convictions about obeying the teaching of Scripture.

What happened in the 20th Century?

Do you enjoy watching the old black and white movies? It is a remarkable fact that these movies, almost without exception, show the women wearing hats or veils in church meeting scenes and often in public. The classic movie "Sergeant York" is an excellent example. In one of the scenes of the movie, a modern day marketer is trying to slick talk a backwoods storekeeper in Tennessee to purchase some highly decorative hats for the women folk. The storekeeper (also the local pastor) informs the salesman that their woman would not be interested because they already wore "split-bonnets." The year is 1916.

In the late 19th century, American women opted for hats in lieu of bonnets and veils worn by European women. Many women in Protestant circles began wearing huge hats, nicknamed "Merry Widows" in the 1890's. Ladies' fashions erupted with provocative styles during the roaring twenties. Women were flaunting more of their skin and hair in public. After a frenzy of fashion changes, the hat was no longer the norm in public attire. By the 1930's women forfeited their hats for the opportunity to show off their long hair. It took only another 20 years before women generally grew tiresome of wearing hats during Protestant religious services. Women in the Roman

33

Catholic churches generally continued wearing veils until the 1970's.

To summarize, in two generations a Christian practice spanning two millennia was generally lost. Apparently, the head covering practice became unfashionable and lost its spiritual significance. In short, Christianity in the early 20th century still maintained the "what" – the head covering, but had generally lost the "why" – the scriptural principle. It is an important lesson for us to pass down to our children. Whenever we don't understand "why" we are practicing something, we ultimately lose the practice. "The why" must be declared to keep "the what"!

Nikodim Kamenskikh from the Urzhum, Kirov province in Russia seems to understand the erosion of Christian behavior when Bible doctrine is neglected. After explaining the importance of women covering themselves in the Russian Churches, he writes: "Just as a large river begins from a small stream, so every violation or neglect begins with something small and almost imperceptible"[46]

The practice of women covering themselves with a veil has been an accepted spiritual exercise throughout the history of the church. Scholars, teachers, and church leaders from the dawning days of the church age to present have explained passionately its biblical relevance and spiritual significance. Presently, only a few groups of Christians still practice this symbolic display of divine order. Will it be possible for Christendom to resurrect this visible symbol of God's order in the church during the 21st century?

Who is Paul's Target Audience?

Before speculating why Paul wrote to the church at Corinth on the subject of head coverings, an understanding of the cultural practices of the day is necessary. By understanding the cultural behavior, it will be possible to determine who was at the focus of his discussion.

Ancient Corinth was located in southern Greece and strategically situated on the trade routes of Paul's day. Its major seaport on the Aegean Sea not only invited enormous commerce, but also a smorgasbord of immoral pleasures to satisfy the base appetite of any visitor. David Lowery writes concerning Corinth:

> In the earliest Greek literature it [Corinth] was linked with wealth (Homer Iliad 2. 569-70) and immorality. When Plato referred to a prostitute, he used the expression "Corinthian girl" (Republic 404d). The playwright Philetaerus (Athenaeus 13.599a) titled a burlesque play *Ho Korinthiastes*, which may be translated "The Lecher." And Aristophanes coined the verb *korinthizaomai* to refer to fornication (Fragment 354). According to Strabo (Geography 8. 6-20) much of the wealth and vice in Corinth centered around the temple of Aphrodite and its thousand temple prostitutes. For this reason a proverb warned, "Not for every man is the voyage to Corinth."[1]

Corinth was the "Sodom" of Greece at the time of Paul's writing. For this reason, it is impossible to unequivocally assert what the particular head covering custom of Corinth actually was. Its city life was out of the norm. It would be like describing the social life of Las Vegas by normal American culture. This is not possible, as Las Vegas is a unique city. The general social behavior prevalent in Las Vegas certainly doesn't reflect small town life in the state of Iowa. Although it is difficult to positively identify the social protocol of Corinth, sufficient historical evidence does exist to declare ordinary Greek, Roman and Jewish practices of the day. It can be assumed that the Corinthian assembly consisted of predominantly Greek believers with a Jewish contingent. Luke records that many of the Corinthians believed the gospel message, including a gentile named Titus Justus who lived next door to the synagogue Paul had been preaching in. Perhaps some Christians from a Roman background were also present. This would proportionately reflect the local population.

Many Jews had settled in Greece after being expelled from Rome by the decree of Claudius in 49 AD. Jewish immigrants from Rome such as Aquila and Priscilla settled in Corinth and were originally a part of the church meeting there (Acts 18:2). Acts 18:4 records that Paul "reasoned in the synagogue every sabbath, and persuaded the Jews and the Greeks." Some time later, after Aquila and Priscilla had moved to Ephesus, they sent a Jew named Apollos to the Christian assembly at Corinth (Acts 18:27 – 19:1). We also know the chief ruler of the synagogue, Crispus, and his family departed from Judaism to follow Christ (Acts 18:8). Based on the historical and scriptural evidence, we can reliably conclude that the believers at Corinth were of a diverse ethnic makeup. It is most probable that Jews, Greeks and perhaps Romans were gathering together in the name of the Lord Jesus amidst the vilest of social backdrops.

What were the Greek social customs concerning headgear? The Greeks practiced several unique customs concerning their hair and headdress. Bruce Terry explains the custom of intellectual men of the day: "The Greek sign of an educated man was wearing of the hat of Hermes as was done by the philosophers.

This yarmulke is still visible under the tasseled mortarboard worn by the graduating classes from education institutions."[2]

Plutarch, a first century Greek philosopher and biographer, describes the Greek practice of mourning at funerals, "So in Greece, whenever any misfortune comes, the women cut off their hair and the men let it grow...."[3] Admetus, ordering a common mourning for his wife Alcestis, says, "I order a general mourning for this woman! Let the hair be shorn off, and a black garment put on."[4] It seems self-evident that women would not be recognized as mourning (i.e. have short hair) if they were always veiled in public. It is noted that their black attire would distinguish them from prostitutes. However, Adam Clarke acknowledges in his commentary on 1 Cor. 11 that the Greek women were inclined to avoid this custom where possible:

> Even in mourning it was considered disgraceful to be obliged to shear off the hair; and lest they should lose this ornament of their heads, the women contrived to evade the custom, by cutting off the ends of it only. Euripides, in Orest., ver. 128, speaking of Helen, who should have shaved her head on account of the death of her sister Clytemnestra, says: Ειδετεπα ρακρα ςωςαπε θρισεντριχ α ςσωζουσα κα λλοςεστιδεηπαλαιγυνη: "see how she cuts off only the very points of her hair, that she may preserve her beauty, and is just the same woman as before."[5]

Plutarch, also asks in the *The Roman Questions*: "Why is it that when they worship the gods, they cover their heads, but when they meet any of their fellowmen worthy of honour, if they happen to have the toga over the head, they uncover?" and "Why do they sacrifice to Saturn with head uncovered?"[6] Greek men normally did not wear anything on their heads while in public or while worshipping, although their Roman and Jewish counterparts normally had their heads covered during worship. M. R. Vincent summarizes the practice of men:

> The Romans, like the Jews, prayed with the head veiled. So Aeneas: "And our heads are shrouded before the altar with a

Phrygian vestment" (Virgil, *Aeneid*, iii., 545). The Greeks remained bareheaded during prayer or sacrifice, as indeed they did in their ordinary outdoor life.[7]

If the reader has viewed the "Jesus Film," you might recall a scene in which a scribe hands the Lord Jesus the scroll of Isaiah. While reading the scroll, the actor playing the Lord is seen with his head covered, but after he completes the reading, he uncovers His head. This scene portrays the Jewish practice of men covering their heads during religious gatherings. Similarly, Roman men and women prayed with their heads veiled.[8]

Greek men and women did *not* worship with a covering on their heads.[9] In discussing the Greek customs regarding women's headdress, Albrecht Oepke writes:

> To be sure, the veil was not unknown in Greece. It was worn partly as adornment and partly on such special occasions as matchmaking and marriage …, mourning …, and the worship of chthonic [underworld] deities (in the form of a garment drawn over the head). But it is quite wrong that Greek women were under some kind of compulsion to wear a veil in public.[10]

What might Greek women wear on their heads when they were so inclined? M. R. Vincent describes a variety of Greek feminine headdressings, "The head-dress of Greek women consisted of nets, hair-bags, or kerchiefs, sometimes covering the whole head. A shawl which enveloped the body was often thrown over the head, especially at marriages or funerals."[11]

The historical evidence does not conclusively suggest that the lack of a head covering in Greece indicated that a woman was a prostitute or had loose morals as it did in the Jewish culture. It is true that perhaps a thousand unveiled vestal virgins (prostitutes) connected with the temple of Aphrodite roamed the streets of Corinth at the time of Paul's writing; however, these women were easily identified by their attire and some had their heads shaved (the basest sort). A Greek woman may or may not cover her head in public, depending upon the event and the occasion. Oepke depicts this point when he quotes Plutarch in *Sayings of Spartans* regarding Charillus, an early king of Sparta: "When someone inquired why they took their girls into public places unveiled, but their married women veiled, he said, 'Because the girls have to find husbands, and the married women have to keep to those who have them.'"[12] Granted this is Sparta, a region of Greece, and not Corinth, but it does indicate that Greek women were at liberty to be in public without a head covering. Thus, Paul's head covering instructions would be quite contrary to their present practice. E. Kasemann concludes, "There remains a considerable consensus that Paul was trying to establish something foreign to Greek culture in Corinth."[13]

Additionally, James B. Hurley acknowledges that several drawings on early Grecian pottery show an absence of head coverings.[14] Concerning church meetings, Paul exhorts the Ephesian women to dress modestly and not to elaborately braid their hair (1 Tim. 2:9). Not only does it show that some women were uncovered in this Asian church, but they were also being influenced by the styles of the local pagan prostitutes.

What was the custom of Jewish women during the 1st century? In New Testament days, Jewish women remained covered in public as well. A Jewish woman was generally considered immoral (a prostitute or an adulteress) if her head was uncovered in public. If she were a prostitute, the gesture of being uncovered was an advertisement to potential clients. The woman who visited Jesus in Luke 7:38 apparently had no head covering. Perhaps in this way she was understood to be a harlot.

The ancient Rabbinic writings of the Talmud contains several references to the woman's head covering, thereby validating its existence. The Talmud states "The sight of a woman's hair constitutes an erotic stimulus" (Berakhot 24a). "Jewish women, married or not, should not walk in the marketplace with their hair uncovered" (Shulhan Arukh, Even ha-Ezer 21:2). Jewish women were not to go out into public without covering their heads (Bereshit Rab.17; Ket.72b). Some Jewish women, believing that "wives" hair should always be covered (Nash. Ned.30b), wore head coverings in the home as well as in the streets (Yoma 47a; Lev. R.20:11). Some rabbis viewed the head covering so important that they would not utter blessings in the presence of a bareheaded woman (Berakhot 24a). Lastly, a man could divorce his wife for venturing into public with an uncovered head (Kethubah 7:6). 3 Maccabees 4:6 also references the veiling of a Jewish woman. Consequently, not only were Jewish women heavily veiled in public, many women chose to remain veiled at home. Because of these conservative practices the Jewish culture strongly affected women in southern and eastern Asia Minor. The Jewish veiling practices in Paul's day had remained virtually unchanged since their conception as a people. In addition to being a religious practice, the feminine coverings also marked one of the clearest distinctions between the Jewish and Greek cultures.

Albrecht Oepke describes the strict use of the head covering by Jewish women:

> Philo, a first century Alexandrian Jew, describes the head covering (Greek *epikranon*) as a token of modesty which the guiltless use. And it is related that a certain woman named Qimchith, who was the high priest's mother, was always veiled, even in the house.... Evidence of the veil in Tarsus is provided by Dio Chrys[ostom] Or[ationes], 33, 46 and coins bearing the image of Tyche of Tarsus.[15]

John Lightfoot quotes several sources showing that Jewish women were veiled in public, but then writes: "when they resorted unto holy service they took off their veils, and exposed their naked faces; and that not out of lightness, but out of religion." Why did the Jewish men feel compelled to cover themselves during prayer? Again Lightfoot writes, referring to Jewish law, "He should veil himself to show that he is ashamed before God, and unworthy with open face to behold him."[16]

Regarding the veiling of women in Tarsus, William M. Ramsay acknowledges that Dio Chrysostom praises only one Tarsian characteristic:

> ... unreservedly, and that he praises, though it was, as he says, *utterly different from the Hellenic custom* (emphasis added). He was much pleased with the extremely modest dress of the Tarsian women, who were always deeply veiled when they went abroad. As Tarsian ladies walked in the street, you could not see any part either of their face or of their whole person, nor could they themselves see anything out of their path.[17]

Even Tertullian, a century and a half after 1 Corinthians was written, acknowledges the sharp contrast of the veiling practices of Greek and Jewish women in public, "Among the Jews, so usual is it for their women to have the head veiled, that they may thereby be recognized."[18]

To summarize, it was not scandalous for a Greek woman to appear in public without her head covered, though they often covered their heads on special social occasions or as a matter of ornament. Unfortunately, some Christian resources have only added confusion to the issue, by hastily generalizing the multicultural ramifications of Paul's day. For example, one well-known Christian Handbook writes "No decent woman would appear unveiled in public at this time. The veil guaranteed safety and respect in the streets."[19] This would be unmistakably true in the Jewish culture, but not dogmatically so for the Roman or Greek. To make this distinction is relevant, for some have asserted that the true purpose of Paul's teaching was to encourage the Corinthian women not to appear immoral as a prostitute. There is no historical or biblical case for justifying this hypothesis; Paul is addressing the church about spiritual exercise and not social customs. Consequently, Paul does not substantiate the wearing of a head covering based on "cultural" arguments; in fact he refers to "creation" order itself.

Bruce Terry pens a concise synopsis concerning the diverse cultural headdress practices during the time of Paul's writing:

> By way of summary, it may be noted that in the first century among the Romans, both men and women worshipped with the head covered; among the Greeks, both men and women worshipped with the head uncovered; and among the Jews, men covered their heads and women uncovered theirs when they worshipped. Thus Paul is introducing a new Christian tradition, which he grounds, not in the social customs of his day, but in theological arguments. With this background, it is not difficult to see why someone would want to discard the head covering for women in Corinth. "After all," he would say, "women don't have to wear head coverings in pagan or Jewish worship; why should they have to in Christian worship?" Once again, non-Christian culture was clashing with Christian tradition.[20]

Given the cultural dynamics of the day, whom might be the focus of Paul's writing in 1 Corinthians chapter 11? First of all, those who may have been causing division in the assembly over the issue. Given Paul's instruction in 1 Corinthians 14:33-35 concerning proper speaking roles among genders in the church, one can surmise that some women knew the headship/head covering teaching and were not abiding by it. Perhaps some men also. It is likely that some women were flaunting their new Christian liberties by assuming church roles not ascribed to them. Their rebellious attitude against God's creation order was in direct conflict with the symbol of submission they had been instructed to wear to show God's order. History has shown that when one aspect of Scripture, such as the head covering practice, is ignored it then becomes easier to ignore other teachings of God's word. Once the snowball starts rolling down the hill, it gains momentum and mass until, humanly speaking, nothing can stop it. Finally, an apostate church is realized.

Secondly, perhaps Paul was speaking to those who did not advocate peace on the issue and were needlessly offending other believers from a different cultural mindset. The mature believer would be longsuffering until Paul could give further specific teaching and/or rebuke on the matter. A mature believer would give the younger ones in the faith time to understand the nature of headship truth and for the Holy Spirit to provide personal conviction.

Thirdly, Paul would be addressing the Greek women who normally did not cover their heads during religious meetings. He was directing the Greek women to follow the Jewish practice of covering, contrary to their normal religious custom. However, he would also be directing Jewish women not to remove their coverings during spiritual exercise. Paul was urging the Greek women to change from their former practice only when "praying and prophesying," not in their public attire. The same can be said for the Jewish women who covered themselves in public.

The covering used by Jewish women is thought by many commentators to have been a large piece of cloth that was a common article of clothing such as a shawl or cape. The cloth would be available as a head covering at any time it was appropriate. Paul most likely had this cloth in view when writing 1 Corinthians. Paul was a Jew himself and from Tarsus, where the customary head covering worn by women in public was Jewish in nature. It is also significant to note that the Hebrew word for "veil" (Radid) and "subjection" (Radad) have close root connections. Thus, Paul did not introduce some new covering with a peculiar spiritual significance, but simply reapplied what was already customary in Jewish circles.

Fourthly, Paul was directing Jewish and Roman men to follow the custom of the Greek men, who remained uncovered during church meetings and while praying and prophesying. This would be difficult instruction for Jewish men who worshipped and prayed with a covering called a *tallith* on their heads. Adam Clarke summarizes this point: "This decision of the apostle was in point blank hostility to the canons of the Jews; for they would not suffer a man to pray unless he was veiled."[21]

So whom was Paul addressing? Likely a wide range of folks. He was speaking to those who knew the truth and were ignoring it or using it to cause division within the church, and also to those who were innocently ignorant of the truth or didn't understand the symbolic nature of the head covering practice. Consequently, the only two groups of people representing divine order properly in the church were Greek men and Roman women.

It can be reasonably concluded that there was not a uniform practice regarding women's headdress in the first century Roman Empire. In public and in the church, the practices were diverse and along cultural lines. Paul had been summoned to sort out the discrepancies in practice. His direction, as described in 1 Corinthians chapter 11, was not specific to the Greek, Roman or Jewish practices. Paul did not appeal to the social customs of the day or Jewish law in his arguments for women to cover themselves and for men to be uncovered. His divinely inspired explanation would be based on symbolic truth illustrating creation order. There would be no cultural ties – thus his Apostolic charge would be a real shocker to all of them.

Why was Paul Writing?

Ephesians is a letter that addresses the mysteries and blessings of the universal church – the body of Christ, while 1 Corinthians centers on the order of the local church. It is evident from Paul's epistles to the Corinthians that there was a central body of truth concerning church order which he was expounding to all local churches – not just those gathered unto the Lord in Corinth:

*Unto the church of God which is at Corinth, to them that are sanctified in Christ Jesus, called to be saints, **with all that in every place call upon the name of Jesus Christ our Lord**, both theirs and ours* (1 Cor. 1:2).

*For this cause have I sent unto you Timotheus, who is my beloved son, and faithful in the Lord, who shall bring you into remembrance of my ways which be in Christ, as **I teach every where in every church*** (1 Cor. 4:17).

*But as God hath distributed to every man, as the Lord hath called every one, so let him walk. **And so ordain I in all churches*** (1 Cor. 7:17).

*For God is not the author of confusion, but of peace, **as in all churches of the saints**. Let your women keep silence in the churches: for it is not permitted unto them to speak; but they are commanded to be under obedience, as also saith the law* (1 Cor. 14:33-34).

> *Beside those things that are without, that which cometh upon*
> *me daily, **the care of all the churches** (2 Cor. 11:28).*

Paul did not have different church truth for different local assemblies; he did, however, have resolute exhortation for those not adhering to revealed Church order. He understood that when God's people disregard divine order they soon devalue God, enter into spiritual decline, and ultimately suffer chaos.

Throughout the First Corinthian epistle, Paul labors diligently to restore "order" in a church that was abusing proper order. In chapters one and three, he exhorts against cliques and disabling divisions in the meeting. Chapter 5, from the onset, rebukes immorality in the church, and chapter 10 addresses eating at the table of demons instead of the Lord's table. Within chapter 11, he deals with the discrepancy of the head covering practice and disorderly conduct at the Lord's Supper. Paul stresses unity within the local church and that all spiritual gifts are important to the body in chapter 12 and then levies practical instruction about using these gifts in love in chapter 13. He addresses proper audible order in the assembly in chapter 14. And finally, chapter 15 is dedicated to refuting doctrinal error concerning the resurrection of Christ (which seemed to have been splitting the assembly). Paul has set forth, in the 1st epistle to the Corinthians, a monumental effort to address both proper personal conduct and the good functioning order of the local assembly.

In the last chapter, it was concluded that the public veiling of women was primarily an Eastern or Oriental custom and was not a forced custom in the West. Although Greek and Roman women often wore a covering as an ornament or for some special occasion, it would be wrong to think that they were under some sort of compulsion to be veiled in public. Roman women did cover their heads during times of worship. It was also shown that Jewish women were commonly veiled, even in the West, but took their coverings off to worship. In addition to this cultural diversity, Roman and Jewish men covered their heads to worship, while Greek men remained uncovered. This was likely the reason difficulties had arisen within the church of Corinth. The Greek and Jewish cultures were clashing in the assembly, and Paul had been summoned to encourage peace by standardizing the practice of covering. Perhaps this church issue had been relayed to Paul personally by Chloe (1 Cor. 1:11) or by the church itself in their letter of inquiry to Paul (1 Cor. 7:1).

Was the head covering teaching in chapter 11 new revelation to the Corinthian church? Not likely. Given the wide range of headdress practices in the church and the fact that Paul had been in Corinth for 18 months nearly ensures that the subject would have been previously addressed. It is likely that some were not following the instruction on the subject they had already received, thus the corrective "but" in verse 3 of chapter 11.

Besides the inherent cultural clashing on the practice, apparently there was still confusion among the Corinthian believers about the purpose and practice of head covering. A. R. Fausset summarizes, "The Corinthian women, on the ground of the abolition of distinction of sex in Christ, claimed equality with men, and, overstepping propriety, came forward to pray and prophesy without the customary headcovering."[1] But was the whole church confused about the practice or were some in line with previous teaching? Because the matter had been made known to Paul in Ephesus, it nearly ensures that some in the church understood the proper teaching. Yet, there was a contingency of women that were set upon elevating their newfound Christian liberty above the practice of symbolic truth in the meetings. Paul would once again, in writing, and perhaps in more detail explain creation order and how it was exemplified through bareheaded men and covered women.

Praise, Ordinances, and the "But"
(Exposition on 1 Cor. 11:1-2)

Be ye followers of me, even as I also am of Christ. Now I praise you, brethren, that ye remember me in all things, and keep the ordinances, as I delivered them to you (1 Cor. 11:1-2).

D. L. Moody once quoted an old preacher who said that "the cries of neglected texts were always sounding in his ears, asking why he did not show how important they were."[1] Unfortunately, 1 Corinthians 11:2-16 is one of the most neglected texts of Scripture. Most modern day preachers shrug it off as out of date cultural bias, spiritualize the meaning away, or simply detour around it as some theological minefield to be avoided. Seldom is an honest, literal and contextual explanation given of this passage. Let us not neglect it any longer.

Paul directly precedes the head covering discussion in chapter 11 with three wonderful principles of "Christian liberty" in the latter portion of chapter 10. Through teaching Christian liberty Paul softens their hearts to better receive the forthcoming rebuke. He reminds them that their liberty in Christ should not hinder their spiritual growth (v. 23), but should glorify God (v. 31) and *"give [no] offense, neither to Jews, nor to the Greeks, nor to the church of God"* (v. 32). Where Scripture was silent, these principles would help guide their behavior as to what was permissible. Certainly, the attitude of avoiding needless personal offense would be a crucial mindset for the Corinthians given the forthcoming head covering discussion.

With this statement, Paul begins a new subject in his letter to the Corinthians. Chapter 11 commences with exhortation to following apostolic teaching: *"be ye followers of me, even as I also am of Christ"* (v. 1). Paul even praises the Corinthians for "holding fast" to the ordinances he had *"paradidomi,"* which means "delivered or committed" to them (v. 2). It is quite possible, based on the phrase *"I would have you know"* in verse 3, that Paul was praising these Christians for obeying his teaching even though they didn't fully understand the principle underlying it. It is commendable for all Christians to behave in this manner – obey simply because it is a precept of Scripture. Christians, as indicated by the use of the word "brethren," are requested to remember what was handed down from God, by the Apostles to us. Even today, believers should be encouraging one another to seek the Holy Oracles of God for counsel and direction in life. The same Scripture Paul was referring to has been "delivered and committed" unto us also in the 21st century. Let us not neglect it.

Paul limits his praising to one verse then quickly addresses two areas of improper conduct. The Corinthians were neglecting some of the Apostolic teaching that had been given to them. The more serious matter – their abuse of the Lord's Supper – he saves until later. Instead, he concentrates first on the lesser issue which consisted of two problems: first, the matter of women speaking and praying in a mixed assembly, and secondly, the matter of the head covering practice. He addresses the head covering immediately since it is more relevant, and in chapter 14, he imparts instruction concerning women praying and speaking publicly in a mixed church gathering.

The word "ordinance" in verse 2 can legitimately be translated "tradition." In a bad connotation, the word "tradition" conveys the thought of human opinions and customs being kneaded into church order and teaching. Surely, you have heard some say, "We've always done it like this" in response to a question concerning a particular church practice. This is not the type of tradition that Paul is speaking of. It is not human-manufactured church traditions that are in view, but divinely inspired apostolic tradition. Paul clearly defines what these traditions included when writing to the church at Thessalonica. He commands the Christians to hold to the traditions which they were taught and to withdraw from every brother who did not walk according to the tradition which they received from the apostles (2 Thess. 2:15; 3:6; 3:14). Before the New Testament Scriptures were canonized, the apostles conveyed truth to the early church orally. So if the "tradition" was not the written or oral teaching of the Apostles, it did not need to be followed. However, in the case of the head covering, Paul clearly uses "ordinance/tradition terminology." The doctrine of head coverings may be a minor ordinance in our own eyes, but it is an apostolic tradition and cannot be ignored. As Paul demonstrates in chapter 11, to keep *most* of the traditions brings some praise, but also ensures the instructive or perhaps corrective "but" that begins verse 3.

What is Headship?
(Exposition on 1 Cor. 11:3)

But I would have you know that the head of every man is Christ, and the head of the woman is the man, and the head of Christ is God (1 Cor. 11:3).

How much time do you expend each day in learning how to breathe, or to eat, or to sleep? Hopefully, none! These activities are elementary to us and do not need to be learned again and again, unless there has been mental or physical injury to the body. This is the sense in which Paul is explaining the principle of headship in verse 3. The word "know" (*eido*) means to perceive or discern in the *perfect* tense. Paul wants them (and us) to once and for all discern this truth about headship – it should never have to be relearned.

It is obvious from the context of the passage that Paul is referring to authority and not to physical heads on bodies. The teaching focuses on the subject of position and submission within God's created order. This concept of biblical headship must be understood before venturing into a study of the head covering. Without headship, the head covering is meaningless from a spiritual point of view, because without understanding the truth of headship, the symbol has no power to visibly declare the truth it stands for. Previously, we have discussed the cultural practices among the genders in Paul's day, but not the positional order among the genders from the first day. There is both a positional order and a relational order within God's creation.

Positional order has at its pinnacle, God, then it descends to angelic beings, humanity, animals and the rest of nature (Heb. 1:6-8; 2:6-8; Gen. 1:28-29). In positional order, God and Christ are equal, and the man (reflecting all of the male gender) and the woman (reflecting all of the female gender) are equal. Yet, in relationship order, Jesus Christ (the Son of God) is in subjection to His Father. It is paramount to understand that Jesus Christ is not inferior to God the Father in any way, but He is in submission to the Father. His submission serves as the ultimate example for all believers to pattern their lives after. Jesus Christ is the head of the Church – the supreme authority of all Christians (Eph. 1:22; 4:15; Col. 1:18). Thus, the Christian must submit to Him and the various delegated authorities He has arranged over us. In the same way that Christ demonstrates subjection to His Father, the woman is to be in subjection to the man. Subjection is not an affront to equality, but the splendor of divine order.

Submission to authority and role are vital components to any devised order. Can you imagine the chaos that would follow if proper order were not followed in our society? What if people decided traffic signals were to be completely ignored for the sake of expediting travel? What if everyone decided that waiting lines at amusement parks, sporting events, the post office and checkout stands were to be ignored to ensure the quickest possible conclusion of the matter at hand? Normally, one picks up a phone directory knowing that within moments the name, address and telephone number of anyone being searched for will be obtained. However, what if Mr. Johnson, Mrs. Smith, Miss Jones complained to the phone company about being listed in the middle or towards the end of the telephone directory and demanded to be listed on the first page of the publication next year. Before long, order would be lost, and the usefulness of the directory would be forfeited. Our whole society is based on submission to the order that has been invoked through civil law and social norms. Order is necessary for productivity and blessing; thus, order is at the center of God's nature. *"For God is not the author of confusion but of peace"* (1 Cor. 14:33).

Submission to order includes dependency on the authority over you. God funnels blessings from heaven through proper channels of authority. All of us are under some authority. Since the days of Noah, this has been His tool for teaching human submission to Himself. The church is dependent upon Christ for provision and blessing. The Lord Jesus, during His earthly ministry, was dependent upon the Father. A wife is to be dependent upon her husband to provide for her needs and to protect her.

Consequently, the term "head" (in verse 3) refers to someone who has authority and, thus, the one to whom subjection is to be yielded. G. Morrish states that this meaning is in keeping with the Jewish use of the term in the Septuagint and in the other passages of the New Testament.[1] According to the American Heritage Dictionary, the term "headship" simply refers to "the position or office of the head or leader."[2] This is the general explanation of headship, but its application includes many different spheres of authority. The Bible acknowledges proper headship within three main dimensions of authority: church order, home order, and civil order. Each of these spheres, however, should be in adherence to the overall divine order Paul has just spoken of in verse 3 if the maximum blessing of God is to be obtained.

In "home order," wives are to be submitted to their husbands (Tit. 2:5; 1 Cor. 11:3; Col. 3:18; 1 Pet. 3:1; Eph. 5:22-23; Gen. 3:16). Positionally, the wife is equal to her husband, yet God has given the husband authority over the wife in the marital relationship. It was God who initiated the marriage relationship in Genesis 2:23-24; therefore, His rules apply. He has put a proper order in place, one that in Matt. 19:5-6 the Lord Jesus reconfirms has not changed. God does not change (Mal. 3:6; Heb. 13:8); therefore, his order for family life does not change either. Paul explains the "why" of family order in 1 Tim. 2:11-14:

Let a woman learn in silence with all submission. And I do not
permit a woman to teach or to have authority over a man, but
to be in silence. For Adam was formed first, then Eve. And
Adam was not deceived, but the woman being deceived, fell
into transgression (NKJV).

Just prior to explaining why the first man was placed in
authority over the first woman, the general principle of headship
is presented in verses 11 and 12. Adam was created first, and the
woman was created from Adam. Therefore, the woman cannot
be superior to one that she was taken from. Secondly, the woman
was deceived when Satan tempted her, thus proving that she was
not a fit leader for the marital union. Adam, however, sinned
with his eyes open. He knew it was wrong, but was inclined to
follow his wife's lead.
William MacDonald comments on verse 12 of this passage:

Neither is a woman to have authority over a man. That means
that she must not have dominion over a man, but is to be in
silence or quietness. Perhaps we should add that the latter part
of this verse is by no means limited to the local assembly. It is
a fundamental principle in God's dealings with mankind that
man has been given the headship and the woman is in the
place of subjection. This does not mean that she is inferior that
is certainly not true. But it does mean that it is contrary to
God's will that the woman should have authority or dominion
over the man.³

Concerning "Civil Order," God never anointed a woman to
be a national prophet, priest or king in Israel. Perhaps Deborah,
at a quick glance, would be the closest breech of this statement,
but a more detail observation reveals several important aspects
of Deborah's ministry. J. Hunter notes:

It must be stressed that her [Deborah's] judgeship was
different from that of the male judges. Judges 2:18 brings
before us three characteristics concerning judges: firstly, the

Lord raised them up; secondly, His presence was with them; thirdly, God delivered Israel out of the hand of their enemies all the days of the judge. Of Deborah, Judges 4:4 says she judged Israel "at that time." The previous verse (v. 3) explains this expression. She judged Israel during the "twenty years he (Sisera) mightily oppressed the children of Israel." She judged during the time of bondage, whereas the male judges delivered Israel and ruled over them. Verse 5 then informs us that the children of Israel came to her for judgment, thus availing themselves of her knowledge, wisdom and discernment. When the time came to deliver Israel, God used Barak in the public action and victory, although he was inspired by Deborah. Note also in Heb. 11:32 it is Barak that is named.[4]

So, was Deborah a national leader? No. Deborah imparted wisdom and judgment on an "individual" basis for those who came to her for counsel. She was not a "national" deliverer like the other judges – she did not lead the army into battle against the Canaanites. She herself understood her calling and, thus, encouraged Barak to lead the campaign.

Lastly, "Church Order" also reflects the divine order of headship. Only men were called to be Apostles of the early Church, and only men qualify to be church leaders (elders) of the local assembly (Tit. 1:6; 1 Tim. 3:1-2). Only men are to be duly appointed to the office of deacon in the local church (1 Tim. 3:11-12; Acts 6:3). Only men are to speak in public meetings of the church (1 Cor. 14:34; 1 Tim. 2:9-12). It is not to say that women are not important to the church, for many are mentioned in Scripture as being helpers, encouragers, and even teachers. But what did they teach and to whom? Women taught other women and children in domestic issues of life (Tit. 2:3-4; 2 Tim. 1:5; 3:14-15).

J. Allen emphasizes that there is grammatical evidence to properly translate verse 12 as "I permit not a woman to be a teacher."[5] K. Wuest, known for his expanded translation of the

Bible, mentions the same grammatical support concerning this verse:

> The kind of teacher Paul has in mind is spoken of in Acts 13:2, 1 Cor. 12:28-29, and Ephesians 4:11, God-called, and God equipped teachers, recognized by the Church as those having authority in the Church in matters of doctrine and interpretation.[6]

Women were not to exercise authority over men, nor were the sisters to teach the brothers doctrine. Perhaps one of the best illustrations of this headship principle in the early church is the narrative account of Paul's return to Jerusalem in Acts 21.

Paul was refreshing himself in the home of Philip for a few days before traveling to Jerusalem. Acts 21:9 records the fact the Philip had four virgin daughters who did prophesy. Although it is true that these women had the gift of prophecy, there is no evidence they ever used this gift in the church meetings. Prophecy is not limited to church meetings any more than prayer is. It should also be pointed out that God used an older male prophet, Agabus, who had to travel some 40 miles to exhort Paul, instead of using Philip's daughters who were not only in the same city, but within the same house that Paul was staying. It would have been much simpler to have one of Philip's daughters rebuke Paul; instead, God summoned Agabus. This demonstrates the principle of divine headship. It would have broken God's order to have a woman instruct the Apostle. The fact that prophecy is not constrained to the church meeting is apparent in that Agabus prophesied to Paul outside of a church meeting.

The thoughts of C. H. Mackintosh will conclude our discussion on the women's role in God's order:

> In conclusion, then dear friend, we would just express our ever deepening conviction that *home* is, pre-eminently, the woman's sphere. There she can shine whether as a wife, a mother, or a mistress, to the glory of Him who has called her

to fill those holy relationships. There the most lovely traits of female character are developed – traits which are completely defaced when she abandons her home work and enters the domain of the public preacher. We believe it is plainly opposed to Scripture for a woman to speak in the Church, or to teach, or in any way, usurp authority over the man. But if there be a meeting of a private, social character, there is, in our judgment, an opening for the free communication of the thought, provided always that the woman keep the place assigned her by the voice of nature and the Word of God. [7]

Note that Paul says Christ is the head of "*every* man" in verse three. This is important since Paul is writing to a multicultural church containing Greek men who normally did not cover their heads while worshipping. So how would the uncovered heads of men and the covered heads of women visibly promote the truth of God's headship?

Every woman who willingly covers her head personally declares:

1. I acknowledge male authority in God's plan and, thus, will not use any means, such as beauty, flattery, or any form of manipulation, to control men (1 Pet. 3:1-4).

2. I will submit to God by submitting to the male authority over me knowing that it is God's means to care and provide for me (Rom. 13:1-2; 1 Pet. 3:5-7).

3. I will no longer listen to or be deceived by Satan's lie that equality is a thing to be grasped, for indeed order has already been settled by divine authority (Gen. 3:4-5; Phil. 2:5-6).

It should be emphatically noted that forcing the head covering practice mocks the divine reality of headship. What other aspects of Christian activities are forced? Baptism? The Lord's Supper? Prayer? Giving? The answer is none. If the mind does not understand headship, or the associated veiling practice to demonstrate this truth, a woman should not be forced to practice it. God wants a spirit of submission to truth, not bitterness. Room to breath and time for the Holy Spirit to convict is always the better route to go than brow beating and guilt trips! With this said, a woman who understands the practice and will plainly not submit to it is another matter. Each situation must be reviewed and judged by the elders. Certainly, such a woman should be limited from any visible role such that her appearance would mock God's order and undermine the church's position (such as teaching Sunday School). What if the woman is divisive about the issue? In such a case, 2 Thess. 3:6, 14 and Rom. 16:17 seem to clearly apply and some form of church discipline should be invoked if rebuke has not achieved a change in behavior. The same procedure would be employed for a man who would not want to remove his cap in the church meetings.

Every man who willingly maintains his head uncovered personally declares:

1. I will not rule by my own wisdom or for my own honor and glory, but by seeking God's wisdom and glory in what I do (Luke 16:15; 1 Cor. 3:18-19).

2. I will reflect God's righteous authority in the way I lead (1 Cor. 11:3-5).

3. I will be a self-giving instrument of Christ's love and provision to all those who are under my authority, demonstrating to them the character of Christ (Eph. 5:25; 1 Tim. 5:8).

Consider Matthew Henry's summary of Paul's teaching on headship, including the necessity of the veil as a visual reminder of God's order:

The man that prays or prophesies with his head covered dishonoureth his head, namely, Christ, the head of every man (v.

3), by appearing in a habit unsuitable to the rank in which God has placed him. Note, we should, even in our dress and habits, avoid every thing that may dishonour Christ. The woman, on the other hand, who prays or prophesies with her head uncovered dishonoureth her head, namely, the man, v. 3. She appears in the dress of her superior, and throws off the token of her subjection. She might, with equal decency, cut her hair short, or cut it close, which was the custom of the man in that age. This would be in a manner to declare that she was desirous of changing sexes, a manifest affectation of that superiority which God had conferred on the other sex. And this was probably the fault of these prophetesses in the church of Corinth. It was doing a thing which, in that age of the world, betokened superiority, and therefore a tacit claim of what did not belong to them but the other sex. Note, the sexes should not affect to change places. The order in which divine wisdom has placed persons and things is best and fittest: to endeavour to amend it is to destroy all order, and introduce confusion. The woman should keep to the rank God has chosen for her, and not dishonour her head; for this, in the result, is to dishonour God. If she was made out of the man, and for the man, and made to be the glory of the man, she should do nothing, especially in public, that looks like a wish of having this order inverted.[8]

What would happen to an army if the soldiers holding the rank of a "private" suddenly started wearing "stripes" of a higher rank and then demanded the authority of that rank – say a captain? First of all, the army would be in total disarray and would be unable to accomplish military objectives. People not qualified to issue orders would be interfering with and contradicting those individuals who actually had the proper rank and instructions from "high command." Secondly, those who proudly assert to the higher rank would be severely punished by those in high authority. This adequately describes what was happening in Corinth and what still occurs in many churches today. There were women who were seeking higher rank in the church meeting than what the Supreme Authority had given them. These women had also thrown off their symbols of rank. What was the result? Confusion characterized the church meetings (1 Cor. 11:17-34; 14:23-26), and the chastening hand of God was being invoked upon them (1 Cor. 11:30).

Do we want our church meetings to be characterized by chaos and God's discipline? Surely not. Then let us obey God's command on this matter of headship and its associated symbol of submission to rank – the veil. Let all things be done to edify and build up the church (1 Cor. 14:26). God is not a God of disorder, but desires peace in the churches (1 Cor. 14:33). Peace, spiritual growth and order are integral qualities of church harmony. Let's do our part to maintain these aspects of church life so that we might enjoy our church meetings and relish the fact that we are pleasing God in doing so.

> I am a woman, not a man,
> > created second in God's plan.
> To find what role in life I play,
> > I read God's word every day.
> I find content that I must be
> > to let a man rule over me;
> This does not mean that in this life,
> > I'm unimportant as a wife.
> My husband needs me by his side.
> > To be his "helpmeet," I take pride.
> As a mother, I gladly share
> > my time, my love, and tender care.
> So many tasks are mine to give,
> > they're never finished while I live.
> God's plan for womanhood is good;
> > I wouldn't change it if I could.

Lois Patterson

The Glory of Divine Order
(Exposition on 1 Cor. 11:4-9)

Every man praying or prophesying, having his head covered, dishonors his head. But every woman who prays or prophesies with her head uncovered dishonors her head, for that is one and the same as if her head were shaved. For if a woman is not covered, let her also be shorn. But if it is shameful for a woman to be shorn or shaved, let her be covered. For a man indeed ought not to cover his head, since he is the image and glory of God; but woman is the glory of man. For the man is not of the woman, but the woman of the man. Nor was the man created for the woman, but the woman for the man (1 Cor. 11:4-9; NKJV).

Verse 4

Every man praying or prophesying, having his head covered, dishonors his head (NKJV).

Perhaps one of the leading reasons for human confusion concerning the head covering passage is the Greek words used to express "the head covering." The normal noun for "veil," *katapetasma*, is not found in this text at all. Instead, the Holy Spirit chose to use a participle or another part of speech. In verse 4, the Greek phrase *kata kephales echon* literally means "having down over one's head" a covering. The noun form of the word "veil" is omitted, but the literal meaning of the "covering" is clearly understood. Similarly, if someone said, "she nursed her baby," it would be understood that a *mother* was the subject of the conversation. The Greek expression then would hardly refer to a man wearing long hair. In fact, Plutarch uses a very similar expression "having the cloak down on the head" to refer to a man pulling his cloak up over his head.[1]

Several Translations of the New Testament reflect the literal meaning of the Greek phrase used to describe a covering (anything put over the head).

> Every man who has *something* on his head while praying or prophesying, disgraces his head (NASV, 1971).

> Every man praying or prophesying, having *anything* down over his head shames his Head (The Interlinear Bible, 1976).

> Every man praying or prophesying, having **[anything]** on his head, puts his head to shame (Darby Translation, 1871).

> Every man praying or prophesying having *anything* on his head, shames his head (Tyndale Translation, 1534).

> Every man praying or prophesying having *anything* on his head shameth his head (Geneva Translation, 1557).

What is the something or anything? Wuest, in his expanded Greek translation writes, "a shawl hanging down over his head."

Paul reiterates the instruction concerning the head covering from each gender's vantage point. First, he states in verse 4 that "every" man should be uncovered when praying or prophesying, and in the next verse, he instructs "every" women to be covered when doing the same. The Greek word *aner* is used to denote a "man." It may be translated "husband," but it clearly is gender specific. The Greek word used to speak of a "woman" is the word *gune*, which can be translated "woman" or "wife" and is completely gender distinct from *aner*. Unfortunately, a few versions translate *aner* and *gune* in verses 4 and 6 as "husband" and "wife," giving the false impression that only husbands' heads should be bare and that only their wives' heads should be covered. However, this translation undermines the clear teaching of divine order in verse 3. It is not husbands and wives that are in view, but men and women. The uncovered heads of "every" man and the covered heads of "every" woman are to symbolically represent divine order. So given the context of the passage the correct translation of *aner* and *gune* through the entire passage should be "man" and "woman," not "husband" and "wife."

Prophesying, *"propheteuo,"* has several meanings: to speak forth with divine inspiration, which may include the foretelling of future events; or simply to utter forth divine truth that has already been revealed through God's written word. In the apostolic age, prior to the canonization of Scripture, God spoke directly through the apostles and prophets to convey truth to His people. Today we understand that a modern day "prophet" would be *forthtelling* truth and not *foretelling* the future. All men approaching God for worship, or for prayer, or to prophesy aloud in the assembly should have their heads uncovered. Their uncovered head represents God and His authority in the assembly. Because of the intercession of our Great High Priest, the Lord Jesus, a believer has free access to the throne of grace and is instructed to come boldly in to God's presence to receive grace in time of need (Heb. 4:14-16).

The Greek word translated "head" throughout the 1 Cor. 11 passage is *kephale.*

Besides literally meaning the head of a person or animal, Thayer's Greek dictionary identifies its metaphoric meaning in Scripture:

anything supreme, chief, prominent
a) used of persons, master, lord: used of a husband in relation to his wife

b) used of Christ: the Lord of the husband and of the ekkle-
sia
c) used of things: the cornerstone[2]

Given the context of the passage and the clear meanings of
the Greek words imposed in verse 4, the understanding of the
verse is derived as "When a man prays aloud or exercises the
gift of prophecy, he is to have his physical head uncovered so
that he would not dishonor himself or his spiritual head, which is
Christ (relating to verse 3)." Likewise, in verse 5, a woman engaging in the same spiritual exercise without her head covered
would dishonor herself and her spiritual head, the man (also relating to verse 3).

John Calvin offers a colorful summary of verse 4:

Paul means nothing more than this – that it should appear that
the man has authority, and that the woman is under subjection,
and this is secured when the man uncovers his head in the
view of the Church, though he should afterwards put on his
cap again from fear of catching cold."[3]

Adam Clarke writes:

Having his head covered – With his cap or turban on, dishonoreth his head; because the head being covered was a sign of
subjection; and while he was employed in the public ministra-
tion of the word, he was to be considered as a representative of
Christ, and on this account his being veiled or covered would
be improper.[4]

Verses 5-6

*But every woman who prays or prophesies with her head un-
covered dishonors her head, for that is one and the same as if
her head were shaved. For if a woman is not covered, let her
also be shorn. But if it is shameful for a woman to be shorn or
shaved, let her be covered* (NKJV).

The Greek word translated "uncovered" in verse 5 is *akata-kaluptos*. The prefix "*a*" means "not," *kata* means "down from or down over," and "*kalupto*" means "hide, cover, or veil;" thus, *akatakalupto* means "not covered down over." This word, less the "a," *katakalupto* occurs twice in verse 6. The literal meaning of *katakalupto* "the act of covering down over" could not possibly refer to affixed hair; there must be a conscious choice, an action by the woman to cover her head. Paul acknowledges the fact that the woman could be "not covered" in verse 6, this would be difficult if her hair was the covering being discussed. Paul further informs us in verse 6, "… but if it be a shame for a woman to be shorn or shaven, let her be covered." It is a shame for a woman to have a bald head (hair shaved off). That is why nearly all women undergoing radiation and chemotherapy treatments for cancer opt to wear wigs or other coverings upon their heads after their hair has fallen out. It is a proper response. The shaving of women's heads was something done to captive women to disgrace them (Deut. 21:11-12). Just as it is a shame for a woman to display a bald head in the physical sense, it is also a shame for a woman to pray uncovered in the spiritual sense; in both cases, the woman should wear a covering.

It would seem that God programmed the human conscience in such a way (Rom. 2:14-15) that morally the woman instinctively knows that she should adorn herself with long hair. Albert Barnes writes:

> Long hair is by the custom of the times, and of nearly all countries, a mark of the sex, an ornament of the female, and judged to be beautiful and comely. To remove that is to appear, in this respect, like the other sex, and to lay aside the badge of her own. This says Paul, all would judge to be improper. You yourselves would not allow it. And yet to lay aside the veil – the appropriate badge of the sex, and of her sense of subordination – would be an act of the same kind. It would indicate the same feeling, the same forgetfulness of the proper sense of subordination; and if that is laid aside, all the usual indications

of modesty and subordination might be removed also. Not even under religious pretenses, therefore, are the usual marks of sex, and of propriety of place and rank, to be laid aside.[5]

Some will argue that verse 15 reads, "For her hair is given to her for a covering," so it is obvious that what covers down over the head is hair. It should be noted that nowhere in Scripture is the term *katakalupto* used to imply hair. If we do assume that *katakalupto* does apply to the hair, we quickly find contextual difficulties in verses 4 and 5. In verse 4, if the covering were hair, men must then pray baldheaded. In verse 5, the fact that a woman has a choice of honoring or dishonoring her head when praying implies that the covering can be quickly put on or put off. How does one remove and reattach hair? Furthermore, if her hair was the covering Paul was referring to in verses 5 and 6 and she removed it (by shaving it off), how could she then be in danger of having her head shaved again? Given the substitution, verse 5 would literally begin like this: "For if a woman does not wear her hair long like a woman ought to, let her be shorn like a man." This makes no sense. For if she were not wearing her hair long, she would already have short hair like a man. The contextual and logical sense of the whole passage and the meaning of the Greek words applied, all indicate a second covering, which could be applied over the natural covering – the hair.

Notice all of the Greek references to "covered" and "uncovered" in the head covering passage are forms of the word *katakalupto*.

Present Participles Passive:
Akatakalupto = uncovered (v. 5)
Akatakalupton = uncovered (v. 13)

Present Indicative Passive Verb:
Katakaluptetai = is covered (v. 6)

Present Imperative Passive Verb:
Katakaluptestho = let (her) be covered (v. 6)

Present Infinitive Passive Verb:
katakaluptesthai = to be covered (v. 7)

Only in verse 15 can one find a direct reference to a "covering," and then an entirely different word than katakalupto is used – *peribolaion. Peri* means "around or all about" and *ballo* means "to cast or throw." Thus, the compound word literally means "to throw or wrap all around." The prefix *peri* indicates the perimeter of something is involved. *Peribolaion* is only used one other time in the New Testament – Hebrews 1:12. It is translated as "vesture" (KJV) or "mantle" (NASV). It was a literal covering about the body. What is the meaning of this wrapped around covering? Long hair worn about the head was the natural covering God intended women to have. It is a fixed covering and, thus, cannot be removed, or put on and off; it is a different covering than Paul referenced in previous verses (which was to be put on during spiritual exercise). *Katakalupto* means "to cover down," while *komao,* translated as "long" in verse 14, literally means, according to Thayer's Greek dictionary, "to let the hair grow." If Paul was teaching "let the woman grow long hair," he could easily have said so by applying *komao* in lieu of *katakalupto*. However, the woman's long hair – the natural covering God gave her – also has a glory attached to it. This glory, the woman's glory, must be covered when she prays or teaches. This action demonstrates the woman's agreement with divine order, her subjection to God, and that she is in no way competing with God's glory.

Some have suggested that Paul was affirming in verse 5 that women could speak publicly in church meetings if their heads were covered. Paul is simply making allusion to another abuse in the Corinthian assembly, women praying and prophesying publicly. He reproves the practice of women speaking during church meetings (i.e. while in the presence of men) in chapter 14. In lieu of confirming this speaking practice, Paul confirmed that a "double error" was occurring in the church – unveiled women were publicly speaking in the assembly. Paul simply states that, even with the Corinthian misconception of appropriate audible ministries in the church, she ought to have had her head covered.

The "double error," speaking in the assembly and being uncovered, was worse than the single error of her head being uncovered.

This "double error" understanding is certainly supported by the Greek words translated "shorn" and "shaven." An uncovered woman in the church meeting was visually declaring, "I want to be like a man" – Paul instructs, "let her be shorn like a man to her shame" (verse 6). This verse addresses the wrong thinking that some have – women need not be covered in church meeting if they don't speak publicly. The Greek word for "shorn" is *keiro*, which means "to use shears to cut the hair short." Paul states that for the offense of being uncovered, (looking like a man) a woman should be shorn (cut her hair short). However, for the double offense of speaking and being uncovered, mentioned in verse 5, the woman was to be "shaved." The Greek word for "shaved" is *xurao* meaning "to shave the hair with a razor." For this insult against God's authority (wanting to look like and lead like the man), she was not only to have here hair shorn, she was to be shaved to her further humiliation. In reality, Paul is not advocating these hair-cutting procedures for women; he simply uses these to make his point – the woman should be visibly covered, thus recognizing God's authority over her.

Concerning the shame aspect of the woman removing her head covering, John Chrysostom comments as follows:

> But if any say, "Nay, how can this be a shame to the woman, if she mount up to the glory of the man?" we might make this answer; "She doth not mount up, but rather falls from her own proper honor." Since not to abide within our own limits and the laws ordained of God, but to go beyond, is not an addition but a diminuation. For as he that desireth other men's goods and seizeth what is not his own, hath not gained any thing more, but is diminished, having lost even that which he had, (which kind of thing also happened in paradise:) so likewise

the woman acquireth not the man's dignity, but loseth even the woman's decency which she had.[6]

John Calvin writes:

Hence we infer that the woman *has her hair given her for a covering.* Should any one now object, that her hair is enough, as being a natural covering, Paul says that it is *not,* for it is such a covering as requires another thing to be made use of for covering it.[7]

When an individual has a personal agenda in the church, eventually they will succumb to twisting Scripture to accommodate their crusade. "The end justifies the means" mentality is always devastating to the church. This manner of thinking was apparent in a recent article appearing in the "religion" section of our local newspaper. A female Methodist pastor in our city wrote an article on the woman's head covering. She proclaimed that the main point of Paul's teaching in 1 Corinthians chapter 11 was simply "that a woman should look professional when she preaches to her congregation." She continued to explain that this was accomplished when a woman "pulled her hair back" instead of just allowing it to hang down naturally. Obviously, this woman is reading from a "holey" version of the Bible. Her exegesis of 1 Corinthians chapter 11 is clearly distorted; she is ignoring qualifications of church leadership (1 Tim. 3:1-2, 11; Tit. 1:6), and the prohibition of women speaking publicly in the church (1 Cor. 14:34; 1 Tim. 2:11-12) and.... What a blessing the church would experience if Christians would just embrace the plain truth of Scripture in lieu of spiritualizing or rationalizing God's words into obscurity. All Scripture was God breathed and given for a purpose (2 Tim. 3:16)!

H. A. Ironside summarizes the matter of the woman wearing a head covering as a simple test of her obedience to God.

Concerning this and other matters it has well been said, "Some things are commanded because they are right, other things are right because they are commanded." "Thou shalt not steal." The commandment did not make it wrong to steal, it was always wrong to steal. "But every woman that prayeth or prophesieth with her head uncovered dishonoreth her head: for that is even all one as if she were shaven. For if the woman be not covered, let her also be shorn or shaven, let her be covered." This is right because it is commanded. God has spoken and it is very often in little things like this that we test our state, whether there is self-will working or whether one is ready to be subject to the Word of God. [8]

Verses 7-9

For a man indeed ought not to cover his head, since he is the image and glory of God; but woman is the glory of man. For a man indeed ought not to cover his head, since he is the image and glory of God; but woman is the glory of man. For the man is not of the woman, but the woman of the man. Neither was the man created for the woman, but the woman for the man (NKJV).

Now the Spirit leads Paul to press the head covering practice by directly connecting the various heads just discussed with manifested glories. The English word "glory" is translated from the Greek word *doxa*, which has a wide application of meanings depending on implication of the text. Some meanings for *doxa* are "dignity," "honor," "praise," "worship," "splendor," "radiance," and "magnificence." However, the best meaning for the general application of the word is "glory." Glory may be defined as "a visible manifestation of an inward nature." The glory of God is the outshining of who He is. The subject matter of verse 7 is that the visible image of man represents God and the glory of God is to be manifested in the authority man has been delegated by God. Why can men be referred to as being the glory of God? Because man was created in God's image. Initially, at

72

creation, man was morally upright and innocent (Eccl. 7:29) and was the crowning finale of God's creative work (Heb. 2:7).

What does the word "image" imply? The Greek word for "image" is *eikon*. The root meaning of e*ikon* is derived from the word *eiko,* which means "be like" or "resemble." According to Strong's Greek Dictionary, the literal meaning of *eikon* is "likeness," but in the figurative sense, as used here, it means "a representation." Our English word "icon" is derived from *eikon*. Icons have become a common part of computer operating systems. The user is able to "click" on an icon to initiate or open a desired program or file. The icon is not the program or file, but is an image that "represents" the program or file. Paul implies by the use of *eikon* that man was made in the moral likeness of God and that man figuratively "represents" God. Adam was not God, but he was an icon representing Him. Adam was a unique creation to this end and, thus, was given a position of authority over creation, including the woman and children.

F. W. Grosheide, former professor of New Testament Studies in the Free University of Amsterdam, explains the association of the word "glory" with the word "image" in verse 7:

> *Glory* does not here have the meaning of the full divine majesty. The word used alongside the word *image* points to that which is not only God's image but also honors and magnifies Him. Man, created last, is the crown of creation (Ps. 8). But this regards the man only, for the woman was created in a way which was different from everything else: she was formed by God from the man. That is why Paul can write that a man, who is the image of God, reveals how beautiful a being God could create, which makes him the crown of creation, the glory of God. A woman, on the other hand, reveals how beautiful a being God could create from a man. Thus Paul makes everything a question of creation.[9]

Boyd Nicholson Sr. comments on the meaning of glory and its tie to man's symbolic representation in creation and his delegated authority from God:

> The glory of a rose bush is the rose. That is not all of the rose bush, but the bloom is the manifestation of its nature. By the rose we learn the nature of the bush. The reason for the uncovered head of the man is given: "Forasmuch as he is the image and glory of God." Image is not likeness; these are distinctly different ideas. *Likeness is similitude,* being like; *image is representation,* whether like or not. The Lord Jesus is never spoken of as "being in the likeness of God." He cannot be "like" God since He is God.
>
> Man must not, then, cover his head in the assembly because he represents God as His image. Further, he is the glory of God. If image is *representation*, then glory is *manifestation*. God's authority must not be hidden. This is the twofold reason for the uncovered head of the man. The woman is not spoken of as the image of man, but as his glory. Here it is not representation, but manifestation. The glory of man must not be manifest in spiritual exercises, therefore that glory must be covered. No glory but God's is to be seen in the spiritual realm. Thus when the man sees the women's heads covered, he is reminded that *his* glory is covered there too. His public ministry is to be done so God alone receives the glory.[10]

It is apparent that Paul is using "heads" and "coverings" as symbols to teach the reality of proper divine order and that there should be visual reminders of mankind's submission to that order. Paul again applies the Greek word *aner* meaning "man," or "husband," and not the general term of *anthropos* for "mankind." The "indeed" in this verse means that all men should "certainly" have their heads uncovered while praying or prophesying. Why? Just as Adam was made in God's image, man today still symbolizes the image of God (His representative) and glory of God (in manifested authority).

Then Paul states that the woman is the glory *doxa* of the man. She is not the glory of God, but she is the glory of man because she was created "from" man. She was not created as a unique original, but from Adam. God did not borrow a design to create Adam. Though the woman is a unique and special creation also, she was taken from man and made for man, and, thus, is his glory. Adam said, "she shall be called woman, because she was taken out of man" (Gen. 2:23). In the same way, children are to be submitted to their parents – for they came from their parents – woman is to be submitted to the man, for she came from him.

Since the woman was created from Adam, she also bore the likeness of God and shared the responsibility of authority over creation as his helper (Gen. 1:26-27; 2:18). However, God does not state that she is the image of the man. She does not, therefore, represent man directly as the man represents God, but displays man's authority visibly. Her very existence gives evidence of man's glory – his authority over creation, including herself. Because the woman was made from the man (v. 8) and for the man (v. 9), God gave the man authority over her (1 Tim. 2:12-13). Thus, nowhere in Scripture do we read that the woman has authority over the man; just the opposite is true (Gen. 3:16; 1 Tim. 2:11-15; Eph. 5:22-23; Col. 3:18).

The glory of God was manifested in the dominion God gave Adam over all things of earth. The man is to righteously emulate and manifest God's nature in the execution of this authority (Gen. 1:26). Adam demonstrated this authority over creation by naming the animals (Gen. 2:19-20). Naming someone or something demonstrates authority over that person or thing. It was a common practice of royalty to demonstrate their claim over captives by renaming them. Joseph was renamed by Pharoah to Zaphenath-paneah, and Daniel was renamed by King Nebuchadnezzar to Belteshazzar. After the fall, Adam would show his authority over his wife by naming her Eve (Gen. 3:20).

John Calvin writes concerning the woman as being the glory of the man:

The woman is a distinguished ornament of the man; for it is a great honor that God has appointed her to the man as the part-ner of his life, and a helper to him, and has made her subject to him as the body is to the head. For what Solomon affirms as to a careful wife – that *she is a crown to her husband,* (Prov. 12:4) is true of the whole sex, if we look to the appointment of God, which Paul here commends, showing that the woman was created for this purpose – that she might be a distin-guished ornament of the man. That the man is the beginning of the woman and the end for which she was made, is evident from the law (Gen. 2:18).[11]

David Dickson, writing in 1659 AD, comments on human representation of symbolic glories:

The man (seeing [he] is the Glory of God, and the representa-tion of his glorious Excellency in respect of the woman over whom [he] is appointed head) ought to [show] forth the Glory of God in his manly deportment: Therefore [he] must beware of this unseemliness in the use of a veil. The woman is the glory of the man, or the image of his dignity, in whom (as in a Glass) the excellency of the man (for whose sake [she] was created) is seen, to whom [she] ought to profess subjection by the covering of [herself]: Therefore seeing the woman behaves herself otherwise amongst you, [she] is blamed for uncomeli-ness.[12]

The role of authority given to the man over the woman is not to be used to suppress or abuse her. The model of true leadership in the Bible is one of humility, selflessness and service. With the authority role, man also has direct accountability with God for his stewardship of whatever overseeing role he has been en-trusted. Concerning family order, this reality was quickly learned by Adam in that although his wife ate the forbidden fruit first – God directed his inquiry to Adam, then held him account-able for his lapse of leadership. Paul explains that though the woman was deceived Adam knew what he was doing was wrong

(1 Tim. 2:14). Church elders will give account of their spiritual leadership to God (Heb. 13:17), and civil authorities will give account to God of their delegated governing responsibilities (Rom. 9:17; 13:1-5).

As the wife submits to her husband, she is submitting to the Lord, for the Lord put her husband in authority over her. God blesses those who are in proper relationship with His authority. In respect to the divine accountability that male authority has, it is somewhat of a liberating position to be born a female. Warren Wiersbe explains this reality for the wife:

> True spiritual submission is the secret of growth and fulfill-ment. When a Christian woman is submitted to the Lord and her own husband, she experiences a release and fulfillment that she can have no other way. This mutual love and submis-sion creates an atmosphere of growth in the home that enables both husband and wife to become all that God wants them to be. The fact that the Christian wife is "in the Lord" is not an excuse for selfish independence. Just the opposite is true, for her salvation makes it important that she obey the Word and submit to her husband. ... joyful submission is evidence that the wife belongs to Jesus Christ.[13]

Summary Statements from Verses 4-9:

1. Men should not cover their heads during times of prayer and teaching because "every" man symbolically represents God and God's authority. The man manifests God's glory in crea-tion.

2. Women should cover their heads during times of prayer and teaching because "every" woman manifests man's authority in creation. Because she was derived from man and created for him, she is to cover herself to ensure man's glory (what came from man) is not in competition with God's glory manifested in the man and to show that the man had prece-

dence in the natural realm. The woman, as steward of the coverings, aids the man in his responsibility.

3. The human conscience instructs a woman to wear long hair as a natural covering and, thus, draws her attention to the need of a spiritual covering while praying or teaching.

4. The passage context, the meaning of the Greek words employed, and the logical sense of the text imply that a second covering is required over the woman's long hair during times of prayer and teaching.

5. While an assembly of God's people are gathered in the presence of the Lord Jesus, God's glory should be seen in the uncovered heads of men, while man's glory – the woman and the woman's glory – her long hair should be concealed. In this way, there are no glories competing with God's revealed glory in the uncovered man. By proper symbolic expression, everyone in the meeting is saying "amen" to God's prescribed order in creation and His rule over them.

Taught by Nature and to Angels
(Exposition on 1 Cor. 11:10-16)

For this reason the woman ought to have a symbol of author-
ity on her head, because of the angels. Nevertheless, neither is
man independent of woman, nor woman independent of man,
in the Lord. For as woman came from man, even so man also
comes through woman; but all things are from God. Judge
among yourselves. Is it proper for a woman to pray to God
with her head uncovered? Does not even nature itself teach
you that if a man has long hair, it is a dishonor to him? But if
a woman has long hair, it is a glory to her; for her hair is
given to her for a covering. But if anyone seems to be conten-
tious, we have no such custom, nor do the churches of God
(NKJV).

Verse 10

For this reason the woman ought to have a symbol of au-
thority on her head, because of the angels (NKJV).

Besides demonstrating agreement with divine order, concealing glories that compete with God's glory, and aiding the man in
remembering his responsibility, Paul introduces another reason
for the woman to cover her head while praying. It is because she
is being observed from the spiritual realm by angels. But why
are the angels observing women? Paul explains in Eph. 3:10 that
God is using the Church as an object lesson – to teach of His
manifold wisdom and abundant grace to powers and principalities in heaven.

The elect angels watched in horror as Lucifer led, with perhaps a third of all created angels, a rebellion against God (Isa. 14:12-15; Rev. 12:4). Without any explanation from God, the elect angels observed the Son of God leave the archways of Paradise to become a lowly man and assume a position in the creation order lower than themselves. From heaven, they gasped as mankind spat into the Savior's face then proceeded to nail Him to a tree. Peter describes the curiosity of the angels and their desire to understand this mysterious offer of God's salvation to humanity (1 Pet. 1:12).

As children, we were occasionally allowed to bring items of interest from home for "show and tell" time at school. Invariably, a snake would be brought by a troublesome lad to scare the girls, while a more sensible girl would bring a lovable puppy to be cuddled by all throughout the day. In the same respect, God is using the church as "show and tell" for all angelic beings. He wants the angels to learn of His matchless grace to humanity. The angels learn the significance of the Lordship of Christ and the place of the Church through the use of object lessons and symbols.

Boyd Nicholson Sr. explains how this is accomplished:

> Just as Aaron is a type of Christ in certain ways, though completely unaware of it himself, and just as the Lord used a little child to teach the disciples a lesson on entrance into the kingdom, although the child was oblivious to his role, so now, though we may be unaware of it, we are under the scrutiny of spirit beings. We are being used by God as object lessons to make known the glorious truths of authority and submission which otherwise would be unintelligible to them. How solemn! Yet Abraham grasped a higher truth when he said, "The Lord before whom I walk."
>
> When a woman comes into a church gathering with her head covered, she performs a ministry to the hosts of heaven. She becomes to angels an object lesson of submission to divine headship. What a rebuke she is to the wicked angels! Their sin

80

is that of rebelling against divine authority. What a delight to the obedient angels, as they see also the man's head uncovered portraying the unshielded glory of God and His accepted authority![1]

The expression "to have power" (KJV) or figuratively "to have a symbol of authority" (NKJV) upon her head is a reference to a covering upon her head. John Lightfoot notes that the expression *"to have power"* denotes "to have *power in* one's own hand, not *a power above* one: as Matt. vii.29; John xix.10; I Cor. vii.37; ix.4; and elsewhere a thousand times."[2]

There has been some debate as to whether the ministry of the sisters through the wearing of a head covering is to fallen angels, or to elect angels, or possibly to both. Bruce Terry provides the following argument from ancient Jewish writing for the case of women ministering to good angels through the practice of the head covering:

> … [a] more likely view is that the angels in question are good angels who are present when the Christians gather for public worship and whose presence demands a certain respect. This meaning is most clearly illustrated by parallels found in the Dead Sea Scrolls. In the Scroll of the War Rule (1QM vii. 4-6) is found:
>
> > And no lame man, nor blind, nor crippled, nor having in his flesh some incurable blemish, nor smitten with any impurity in his flesh, none of these shall go with them into battle … for the angels of holiness shall accompany their armies.
>
> Again, in the "Rule of the Congregation" (1QSa ii. 3-11), also known as the "Rule Annexe" or the "Messianic Rule," is found:
>
> > And let no person smitten with any human impurity whatever enter the Assembly of God. And every person smitten with these impurities, unfit to occupy a place in the midst of the Congregation, and every (person) smitten in his flesh, paralysed in his feet

or hands, lame or blind or deaf, or dumb or smitten in his flesh
with a blemish visible to the eye, or any aged person that totters
and is unable to stand firm in the midst of the Congregation: let
these persons not en[ter] to take their place in the midst of the
Congregation of men of renown, for the Angels of holiness are
[in] their [Congrega]tion.

These two passages, especially the last, remind one of Leviticus 21:17-23. The point is that the holy angels are present in
assemblies for worship (I Corinthians 4:9; Psalm 138:1 LXX).
Therefore those things which are shameful should not be allowed in the assemblies. Now under the New Covenant, being
blind, lame, etc. is not disgraceful, but Paul has just said that
every woman who has her head uncovered while praying or
prophesying disgraces her head; it is just as shameful as if she
had shaved her head. Thus a woman should not pray with her
head uncovered in the presence of angels.

With this understanding, it is possible to see more clearly the
meaning of "authority" in this verse. Ramsay is right in assert-
ing that it is the woman's own authority that Paul is referring
to, but Paul is not here discussing the woman's dignity – in
fact, he is not discussing social customs at all. Rather, he is
saying that since the woman is the glory of man rather than the
glory of God, the head covering is the symbol of her authority
or right to communicate with God. For her to do so without
this symbol of authority is shameful, for this is a sacred time
when angels are present. The last of verse 9 and verse 10 may
thus be paraphrased to read: "Woman was created for man's
sake. For this reason a woman should have a covering over her
head as a symbol to the angels of her right to pray."[3]

John Calvin summarizes the teaching ministry of women to
the angels in this way:

This, therefore, was said by way of amplifying, as if he had
said, "If women uncover their heads, not only Christ, but all
the angels too, will be witnesses of the outrage." And this interpretation suits well with the Apostle's design. He is treating

here of different ranks. Now he says that, when women assume a higher place than becomes them, they gain this by it –
that they discover their impudence in the view of the angels of
heaven.[4]

Harry A. Ironside shares the following personal experience
as a testimony of the "power" that ought to be on the woman's
head.

I spent the first six years of my Christian experience as an of-
ficer in the Salvation Army. In those days I often had occasion
to see how the beautiful little blue bonnet was the power of the
Salvation Army lassie. I remember going into a saloon on the
Barbary Coast in San Francisco seeking the lost. Two of our
Salvation Army lassies appeared, and I noticed that everybody
treated them respectfully and nicely excepting one man, a
half-drunken sailor. When the Salvation Army girl approached
him with her paper, he turned toward her and made a movement as though he would have kissed her, and in a moment as
she drew back five of those ungodly men sprang to their feet,
knocked him down, thrashed him within an inch of his life,
and then threw him out into the gutter for the police. Her bonnet was her power on her head. There were lots of other girls
there, God help them, that nobody would have fought for or
protected. There they were with their brazen faces and uncovered heads, but this little lassie's power was her bonnet.[5]

Verses 11-12

*Nevertheless, neither is man independent of woman, nor
woman independent of man, in the Lord. For as woman came
from man, even so man also comes through woman; but all
things are from God (NKJV).*

In creation order the man and the woman are positionally
equal; they are different only in relationship authority and in representation. The man has a role of authority over the woman, but
this does not make her inferior, just as the Father's role of au-

thority over His Son does not make His Son inferior – They are equal (John 10:30). Man cannot survive without the woman, and woman cannot continue without the man – the genders are mutually dependent upon each other. Woman first came from man, but every man since then has been born of a woman.

David Dickson summarizes the equality of men and women:

> That this comparing of the Man and the Woman, may not [be] drawn out further to the desiring of the Woman, in a *threefold* respect [he] equals the Woman to the Man. *First,* In respect to Christ our Lord, or in respect to our state of Grace in Christ: The Man and the Woman are equal, bought with the same price, and alike ordained to their service of Christ. *Secondly,* In respect to the same Original; for as in the Creation the Woman is of the Man, so by ordinary propagation the Man is by the Woman. *Thirdly,* In respect to the first and principal efficient cause, *i.e.,* God; (who hath made the Man and the Woman, and all things else) the Man and the Woman are equal. [6]

Verses 13-15

> *Judge among yourselves. Is it proper for a woman to pray to God with her head uncovered? Does not even nature itself teach you that if a man has long hair, it is a dishonor to him? But if a woman has long hair, it is a glory to her; for her hair is given to her for a covering (NKJV).*

Paul now commands (imperative phrase) the Corinthians to "judge in yourselves" the matter of women covering themselves. The word "judge" is the Greek word *krino*, which means "to determine, or call in question." Since the letter is written to "all that in every place call upon the name of Jesus Christ" (1 Cor. 1:2) and not just to the Corinthians, it would be good for every Christian to "call into question and make a determination" concerning Paul's question. What is the specific question to consider? What does nature teach? What does the human conscience reveal about God's natural law for displaying femininity properly? Natural law proves that her hair is her glory, her distinguishing mark of femininity, and, therefore, should be covered.

The word "comely" in the KJV is the Greek word *prepo*, which means "what is right, fit, becoming, or seemly." Paul asks the question "is it becoming and proper for a woman to pray uncovered?" The word "uncovered," as explained in the previous chapter, is the Greek word *akatakaluptos*, which means "not covered" or "not down over," and figuratively "unveiled."

Paul confirms the fact that nature, our own conscience, teaches us that a man wearing his hair long is a shame unto him. The word "nature" is from the Greek word *phusis*, which implies distinctive native disposition or constitution of what is right and wrong. Paul informs us that God inscribed into the heart of every person His moral law of what is right and wrong and gave every person a conscience to monitor this information (Rom. 2:14-15). When we have transgressed the known moral law at the spirit level of our being, we feel guilty; this is sin according to James 4:17. Although we don't understand why, we feel guilty when we transgress our conscience. We sense impending judgment though we may not know from whom or why. The fact that the human conscience is invoked proves that we are sinners – that we did not continue in doing what was right (Rom. 2:1-12).

Paul is asking the Corinthians and all Christians to listen to their consciences on this subject of coverings. Exposure to the Word of God sharpens the human conscience in resolution. But here Paul is not asking them to think spiritually about hair length; he simply asks them to examine their natural sense of the matter. Should a man wear his hair long? Should a woman wear short hair? What does nature teach? Clearly, in nations around the world today, where women are not striving for the man's position, long hair is a beautiful mark of femininity. God desires a distinction between the genders. *"The woman shall not wear that which pertaineth unto a man, neither shall a man put on a woman's garment: for all that do so [are] abomination unto the Lord thy God"* (Deut. 22:5).

Not only does the conscience teach the woman that she should have long hair, but then Paul explains that her long hair is also a glory to her – a reflection of the inner nature of her femininity (v. 15). Her hair has been given to her for a natural covering. The word "covering" here as explained in the previous chapter is a different Greek word than used in verses 5, 6, 7, and 13 to speak of a removable covering. The fixed "wrap-round" covering in verse 15 cannot be substituted for the removable "down over the head" covering in verse 5, otherwise a man would need to be bald headed in order not to have anything down upon his head. In fact, *katakalupto* (employed in verses 5-13) never refers to hair in Scripture; it is used to describe something, such as a cloth, which hangs down and covers the head.

The Greek word *anti,* used in verse 15, has caused some to understand that the woman's long hair is an "instead of" covering which replaces the "down over the head" covering (the veil). The word *anti* is found twenty-three times in the New Testament, and in eighteen of those occurrences, the word is used to convey an "instead of" or "against" meaning. When compounded with *hos,* it is translated "because" in Luke 1:20, "therefore" in Luke 12:3, "because" in Luke 19:44, "because" in Acts 12:23, and "because" in 2 Thess. 2:10. This type of meaning is seen in Ephesians 5:31 where *anti* is translated "For – cause." Though some meaning variation of *anti* is noticed, the normal meaning conveyed by the context of the passage is clearly "instead of" or "against." Yet, many, if not most, of literal Bible translations render *anti* in verse 15 as "for" (KJV, NKJV, NASV, ASV). Given the context of 1 Corinthians 11:14-15, the "for" (*anti)* is prompting the reader to compare something *against* something else, but what is to be contrasted? Is the fixed long hair of a woman being compared with the covering "down over" action spoken of in verses 5 and 6, or is the contrast imposed to answer the question presented in verse 13; *"Is it proper for a woman to pray to God with her head uncovered?"* (NKJV).

The context demands the latter option – the long hair of the woman is being compared with the short hair of the man to further identify God's order among genders. J. N. Darby clarifies what the "instead of" covering is in verse 15:

> Finally, the apostle appeals to order of creation, according to which a woman's hair, her glory and ornament, shewed, in contrast with the hair of man, that she was not made to present herself with the boldness of man before all. Given as a veil, her hair shewed that modesty, submission – a covered head that hid itself, as it were, in that submission and in that modesty – was her true position, her distinctive glory.[7]

The contrast is between the short hair of the man in verse 14 and the long hair of the woman, her natural covering, in verse 15. The man's uncovered head was to declare his authority and the leadership he was to have over the woman. The woman's natural covering (long hair) was a natural reminder of her submission to male leadership and compliance with divine order.

Apparently, the Corinthians were confusing gender roles in Church in respect to leadership and public speaking. Leadership ability or possessing speaking gift does not give one the right to lead in or speak in the Church. God's creation order should be at all times visible – this would serve as a constant reminder to mankind and the observing angels of God's supreme authority. Gender distinction and corresponding order was to be highly regarded in the Church. Thus, the woman's long hair of verse 15 served as an "instead of" reminder as compared to the short hair upon the man's head in verse 14. The woman's long hair would be a reminder to be supportive and submissive to the God-ordained male authority over her, as unto the Lord Himself.

Verse 16

> *But if anyone seems to be contentious, we have no such cus-tom, nor do the churches of God (NKJV).*

Paul concludes the head covering instruction with the injunc-tion that the symbolic practice of headship was the normal cus-tom among the churches and should be maintained. By divine inspiration, he was providing a body of Church truth to all the local churches (1 Cor. 1:2; 4:17; 7:17; 14:33-34; 2 Cor. 11:28). The instruction on the head covering was a part of this truth, it was new teaching and did not agree with the Jewish, Roman or Greek headdress customs of the day, but rather timeless creation order.

Because the Greek expressions in this verse have a variety of implications, there have arisen many interpretations of verse 16. It is frankly the most difficult verse in the passage to categori-cally derive. Paul uses the Greek word *dokeo*, which is translated "seem." *Dekeo* means to "think, suppose or be of the opinion of." The word translated "contentious" is the Greek word *philoneikos*, which is a compound word from *philos* meaning "to be fond of or have affection for" and *nikos* meaning "strife." The Greek word for "custom" is *sunetheia*, which means "accus-tomed or a familiar manner." It is the word used in John 18:39 to describe the "custom" of the Romans releasing a Jewish prisoner at the Passover Feast. So what is Paul saying? "If any man sup-poses to be fond of strife over this issue we have no such manner among the churches." Christians should not love contention. Charles Hodge, of Princeton Theological Seminary, summaries verse 16 this way:

> The arguments … having been presented, the apostle says, if any man, notwithstanding these arguments, is disposed to dis-pute the matter, or appears to be contentious, we have only further to say, that we (the apostles) have no such custom, nei-ther have the churches of God. To be contentious, i.e. disposed

to dispute for the sake of disputation. With such persons all argument is useless. Authority is the only end of controversy with such disturbers of the peace.[8]

Paul is not saying that there is no head covering custom in the churches. It would be ludicrous to suggest that Paul would void 13 verses of teaching by one vague comment. He is simply noting that the apostles and all other local churches did not argue about whether or not the sisters should wear a head covering. By implication Paul is giving reproof: "It is only you carnal Corinthians who are fussing about it." It is not God honoring to delay obedience by arguing about what one knows is right; the Bible calls this sin (Jas. 4:17). We may pray for a submitted heart, but personal obedience should not be a matter of prayer, for it is what one does out of love for the Lord Jesus (John 14:15).

Watchman Nee has this to say regarding those who would be contentious about the head covering practice:

> So, for man to be uncovered and woman covered is a charge that only Christian apostles have given. It is a practice the churches of God alone hold, for it is different from both the Jewish and the Gentile custom. It is something new, and it is from God. ... There is no such practice among the apostles of not believing this. If any church does not believe, Paul's answer is, "*We have no such custom, neither the churches of God.*" None of the local churches which the apostles had visited had any such custom as arguing about woman's head covering. So the answer to any who argue is that there is no such practice as arguing about it. ... Therefore, let our sisters cover their heads in the church when praying or prophesying. Why? To manifest that in the church God has obtained that which He has failed to get in the world, in the universe, and among the angels.[9]

But When?

Once an individual has become convinced in his or her own mind that the head covering practice is biblical and relevant throughout the church age, the more arduous question of "when" must be tackled next. When should the brothers uncover their heads, and when should sisters veil themselves? Does the head covering pertain only to "church order?" What about "family order?" The simple answer is "don't venture beyond or stumble short" of the direct teaching of Scripture and let an individual's conscience guide them through all the nuances of implementation.

William MacDonald commenting on 1 Corinthians chapter 11 writes:

> Actually meetings of the assembly do not come into view until verse 17, so instructions concerning the head covering in verses 2-16 cannot be confined to church meetings. They apply to whenever a woman prays or prophesies.[1]

Stephen Hulshizer writes:

> This headship order goes beyond the local assembly gathering, and is applicable whenever, and wherever saints are gathered for spiritual purposes. At such times man is the head of woman in God's order of government in new creation.[2] When does a man need to uncover his head and when does a woman need to cover her head? The answer is, "When the saints are gathered for spiritual purposes.[3]

It is true that headship and the associated symbolic truth of coverings relate to creation order and are, thus, represented by the man and the woman at all times. For example, when Paul instructs Timothy that it is not appropriate for a woman to teach the man or to usurp his authority, the appeal is to creation order not to church order (1 Tim. 2:11-14). Yet the specific instruction of 1 Corinthians 11:5 is not that a woman must be covered at all times or only during church meetings – she is to be covered when she is praying and prophesying. Likewise, the man should be uncovered when he prays or teaches. Certainly, there is no dishonor unto God if a woman, convinced by her own conscience, determines to cover herself at all times. If done with the proper motive and without legalistic pretense, certainly God would be glorified in this submissive behavior – His divine order is reflected at all times.

R. C. H. Lenski writes on this subject of when:

> It is quite essential to note no modifier is attached to the participles to denote a place where these activities were exercised. So we on our part should not introduce one, either the same one for both the man and the woman, for instance, "worshiping and prophesying in church," or different ones, for the man "in the church" and for the woman "at home." But omitting reference to a place, Paul says this: "Wherever and whenever it is proper and right for a man or for a woman to pray or to prophesy, the difference of sex should be marked as I indicate."[4]

When should a woman be covered then relates to when she prays or teaches. The very Scripture, which commands the wearing of the covering also, limits the application to praying and teaching. When might a woman pray? Paul indicates that prayer should be something we are actively doing throughout the day – "pray without ceasing" (1 Thess. 5:17) and "continuing diligently in prayer" (Rom. 12:12). Jesus taught that "man ought always to pray, and not faint" (Luke 18:1). If the woman is not to be hindered in her prayer life, she then has two options: cover herself at all times, or cover and uncover her head at various times throughout the day. For some women, the latter practice can become irritating, but it should be acknowledged that the particular covering itself is not commanded. Angelic beings apply their own wings as coverings; therefore, in application, one's own hand as a covering could suffice if a piece of cloth is not available.

What about prophesying or teaching? Lenski clarifies when and where this prophesying is to occur:

> Paul is said to contradict himself when he forbids woman to prophesy in 14:34-36. The matter becomes clear when we observe that from 11:17 onward until the end of chapter 14 Paul deals with the gatherings of the congregation for public assemblies. The transition is clearly marked: "when ye come together," i.e., for public worship, v. 20. In these public assemblies Paul forbids the woman, not only to prophesy, but to speak at all (14:14-36) and assigns the reason for this prohibition just as he does in I Timothy 2:11, etc.[5]

The simplest and timeless definition of prophecy is to "speak forth the word of God." With this definition, we now ask the question, "why are prophecy and prayer singled out as activities requiring a covered or uncovered head?" What is common to both these activities not common in other Christian practices? One aspect that seems relevant: both prayer and prophecy involve close communion with God. In the one, God is speaking to us through His word (or directly in the early church days), and in the other, we are speaking to God. Perhaps when one is seen to be in direct communication with God through prayer and expressing His word through the power of His Spirit the covering is applicable. The activity itself acknowledges God's intimate presence.

But isn't God omnipresent? Isn't He with us at all times? Yes. However, when we are intimately mindful of His presence in our midst, symbolical representation of His order is required. A general of an army may be present with his soldiers at all times on the battle field, but whenever a soldier ventures into the commander's presence that soldier is still expected to salute and visibly show honor to the authority over him or her. All that would be observing the entrance would understand the soldier's allegiance to the commander. What would happen to a soldier that chose not to visibly show honor to his superior? He would be rebuked and disciplined. Likewise, when God's children seek intimacy with their heavenly Father and Savior, there should be a visual display of respect for God's authority through the displaying of creation order.

When is Christ in the midst of believers? Matthew 18:20 reads: *"For where two or three are gathered together in my name, there I am in the midst of them."* Therefore, when Christians gather for prayer or ministry or for formal church meetings where prayer and teaching occur, the women should be covered and the men uncovered. Invariably, all church meetings will include declarations of revealed truth from Scripture (John 4:24) and the utterance of prayers. These aspects of Christian conduct are certainly present during the Lord's Supper as the church gathers for the specific activity of worship (Luke 22:19-20; Matt. 26:26-27). Though the women would not be praying audibly during the corporate setting, they would be in the attitude of prayer, and their "amen" at the end of each public prayer shows full agreement with what has been uttered.

Is it necessary for women to be covered and men to be uncovered when praying privately? In other words, is it necessary for man's glory (i.e. the woman) and the woman's glory (i.e. her long hair) to be hidden always? As stated earlier, the simple direction of Scripture applies the head covering practice only when prayer and teaching occur. There are, however, indications in the passage that what is in view is a "public" setting. The woman praying with uncovered head dishonors her head – this is refer-ring to both the authority over her and also her own head. Is it a shame for a woman to be baldheaded? If so, it is a shame before others – shame only has meaning in relation to someone else. A bald woman would not experience the shame of others if she were hidden in an obscure location. The same is true if she were praying privately in a room with the door closed (i.e. a prayer closet – Matt. 6:6) uncovered. There would be no shame in this activity because no one would observe her praying.

In other words, is the long hair of a woman a glory to her if it is a complete secret and never seen? Surely what is in view in all these circumstances is something that appears in the sight of men. The term "public" is thus defined as something or an activ-ity which is observed by others. It takes place in the presence of others, and they are aware of it. In reality, unless you are speak-ing out loud, neither humans nor angels know conclusively that you are praying, for the prayers uttered without words have di-rect intercession with God alone (Rom. 8:26). If you are sitting on a park bench with your head bowed and your eyes closed you might be resting, sleeping, meditating, or just daydreaming. The symbol of headship only has significance if others see it. And when is it to be seen? When a woman is known to be praying or teaching. Because God, the General in our illustration, knows the deepest recesses of our hearts, He knows with what attitude we come before Him. Yet those who are observing us drawing near to the Lord in prayer do not know, unless they (man or an-gels) see the visible acknowledgment of submission to God's order.

Whatever line is drawn for the head covering practice among women also defines the counter-practice for men. Would you expect a steel-worker, welding beams 40 stories above the ground, or a coal miner deep under the ground to remove their hard hats to be able to utter a prayer for safety? Of course not, these men can pray within themselves and have direct access to the throne of God whether their heads are covered or not. There is no public shame in this, because no one knows they were praying.

If the command concerning the head covering actually relates to public life only (i.e. there is an awareness by others that someone is praying), the issue of the covering all the time in order to "pray without ceasing" then becomes less constrictive. One may awake and pray during the night without the inhibition of whether a covering should be worn or not. A woman may pray while working in the home without wearing headdress. A woman might pray secretly (not obviously) on a public street without a head covering. Hence, she has not dishonored her head because it is unobserved by others. It is the author's *opinion* that the veil should never be a hindrance to private prayer, but it is to be visible in public environments where praying is known to be occurring. In the church meetings, a woman who bows her head to pray along with the congregation is engaged in public prayer although not audibly. All who witness the head coverings know that the sisters have visibly saluted God's authority and order on behalf of the assembly.

The headship practice has less benefit to onlookers when prayers are uttered privately, but the angels are still taught by it. For private silent praying, where only the Lord and the individual are aware that prayers are being offered, the practice would have minimal benefit as God already knows the meekness of the individual's heart – the covering does not teach God anything. It is possible to wear the head covering in malice, but it is impossible to hide one's heart from God (Heb. 4:13). For such seasons of prayer, each sister must determine how she can best maintain a spirit of humility before the Lord – personal conviction should guide the head covering practice.

Conversely, men should maintain the exact opposite behavior as women in public prayer. All men, whether audibly praying or not, should remove their hats for public prayer. All men, not engaged in audible prayer should bow their hearts in silence and listen to the one speaking on behalf of the assembly at that moment. Our society generally acknowledges the custom of men removing their hats to pray, but not the opposite practice for women. The practice for men was derived from the same passage of Scripture defining the practice for women; yet, it is almost humorous to see saved and unsaved men in various social settings uncover their heads for a public prayer, while the women remain uncovered. The line of appropriate behavior is exactly opposite among the genders. If the men's hats come off, the ladies headdress should be on. Some would make an issue of its being unreasonable for a woman to be ready at all times to put on a covering when prayers are uttered (i.e. having to carry a covering and then putting it on and off). But why should this seem more unreasonable than for a man to remove his hat (with which no one has a problem)?

If the wearing of a head covering is related to private prayer also, we should then insist on a consistent practice concerning both men and women. If the woman is to be covered at all times, the man then must also be bareheaded at all times. Equivalence is demanded by the strength of the passage, but this brings one to a position which is totally impractical and which has never at any point in history been recognized or practiced by the church.

In many realms of our society, such a practice for men would be fatal. Think of sea divers, astronauts, medical professionals, construction workers, soldiers, and those living in polar climates of the earth. Are none of these men allowed to pray because their heads are covered? Is the man permitted to work with his head covered and yet "pray without ceasing?" Then the woman is permitted to work with her head uncovered and allowed to "pray without ceasing." Is the man permitted to lay in his bed with his head covered and pray? Then the woman is permitted to lay in her bed with her head uncovered and pray. Should a woman be hindered from praying while bathing, swimming, or getting a hair cut? Again, whatever boundary lines are drawn for appropriate headdress behavior among women, the behavior for men is automatically defined.

The simplest deciding point of when to cover one's head should be the simple instruction of Scripture – when prayer and teaching are occurring. This is the "safe" understanding of Scripture. There may be some latitude for private praying, in which it is unknown to others that a particular individual is praying. In the author's opinion, there is no shame to an uncovered woman or a covered man who is praying privately – no one else understands the activity. In such areas, an individual's conscience should work the matter out before God with fear and trembling (Phil. 2:12) and not let social issues or the influence of others sway one's own personal convictions, as based on Scripture.

As we have seen, there was a divine purpose for which God instituted the practice of the head covering among those bearing His image. In the same passage that explains the divine purpose, the proper place for the practice is defined also. There are occasions when headdress is not scripturally required for women and is permitted for men. However, for other occasions, namely when the Lord's people engage in prayer and teaching, women should be covered, and men should not. It does not matter if the brothers in the Lord are present only, or the sisters only, or the size of meeting – in all gatherings of spiritual exercise there should be a visible salute to God's order. To this end, the head covering practice is a duty of all Christians.

There is appropriate attire for the work of prayer. It is no different than a mother putting on her apron and taking it off again when the last dirty dish has been washed and put away. The apron is not required at all times, but there is an appropriate time for its use. The woman finds the apron an advantage in "being a keeper of the home." It is the same for the head covering. It may be worn at all times if self-conviction so imposes. There is nothing wrong with reflecting creation order at all times, but this often leads to some guilt as it is simply impossible for a woman to adorn herself with a covering at all times.

Secondly, the head covering should never become "a fair show of the flesh" (to cause glorying in our flesh) which directly

98

undermines the glory of the cross of our Lord Jesus Christ (Gal. 6:12-14). Galatianism (thinking, "I am saved by grace, but I must continue in good doings to earn God's favor and maintain my salvation.") is realized when the head covering becomes a show of superior spirituality to others instead of a humble salute to God's order and authority.

The head covering is not required at all times, but it must be worn by believing women when engaging in the serious work of prayer or while teaching hallowed things pertaining to women and children. In this way, subjection to God-ordained authority is both signified and demonstrated, and the glory of God is evident for all to see. The ministry of the sisters is much like the Kohathities of old – they are "keepers of the covered glories."

Who Should Be Covered?

"I believe in the head covering, but I am not a woman yet," volunteered a 15-year-old. She explained her logic: "I am technically not a woman until I get married, so it is not necessary for me to wear a veil in the church meetings until then." In reality, this innocent perspective was no more than a quest for further understanding. She grasped the teaching, but didn't know how it applied to her. She truly wanted to please God, but was not sure what was required of her. Once "why" and "when" of the head covering practice are understood, the next question often asked is "who," or more correctly "to whom" does it apply? When does a female begin the practice? What is the proper age?

Paul invokes the Greek word *gune* in the 1 Corinthians 11 text, which is a general word referring to a "woman," whether married or not. So it follows that all believing women who understand the headship teaching should apply the associated symbol – have their heads covered. As stated earlier, the practice should never be forced upon women, as this would be an affront to the symbol and mock the essence of headship. Proper headship denotes submission of the will, not just obedience of the body. Obedience can be forced, but submission is a heart issue. The Christian experience should be motivated by love for the Savior and not fear of judgment (1 Jn. 4:18). Thus, the basis for God honoring conduct is a submitted will, not coerced behavior.

So when is a female considered a woman? During Bible times, it was not uncommon for 14 to 16-year-old Jewish daughters to be given in marriage. Consequently, the Jewish bar mitzvah ceremony celebrates a boy's transition to manhood at the age of 13.

There are three Hebrew words which are pertinent to this discussion:

Na`arah (nah-ar-aw') which means "a girl" (from infancy to adolescence): This word is translated damsel, maid (-en), young (woman). It is the word used to speak of Rebekah (Gen. 24:14, 16, 28, 55) and Dinah (Gen. 34:3, and 12).

Yaldah (yal-daw') which means "a damsel, a girl, a marriageable girl." It is used to speak of Dinah in Gen. 34:4.

'Ishshah (ish-shaw') which means "a woman" (used in the wide sense). Abraham's servant uses this word while searching for a bride for Isaac and in reference to Rebakah.

It would seem that the general word employed for "girl" in the Hebrew language could also be applied to an older girl of marrying age, who had not been given in marriage yet. This same individual may also be referred to as a "woman." The poetic description of God establishing a covenant with Israel in Ezekiel chapter 16 is likened to a marriage covenant. God did not make a covenant with a baby girl, but after her "breasts were fashioned." It was obvious that she was a woman that could be married, by the natural manifestation of womanliness in her body (she did not look like a boy any more). Curves, a bust, and menstruation are all natural signs that a girl has become a woman. Rebekah was acknowledged as a woman before marriage. Therefore, it is not marriage that makes a female a woman, but her visual features that clearly define her as womanly.

The Greek seems to support the same conclusion. Mary, the mother of Jesus, is referred to as a virgin in Matthew 1:23. She was probably a 14 to 17 year old girl when she married Joseph. She did not physically consummate her marriage with Joseph until after the birth of Jesus. The Greek word for virgin is *parthenos* (par-then'-os), which means a virgin who is of a marriageable age. Yet we read that "Jesus was born of a woman"

(Gal. 4:4). She was called a woman before ever experiencing a sexual union with Joseph.

Since the head covering is to conceal man's glory (the woman), it would seem pertinent that girls start to cover themselves when they start to understand this truth and acknowledge God's role and purpose for them. Though unlikely, it is possible that a young girl may choose to reflect divine order by covering herself during the church meetings even before she has believed the gospel message and received the gift of salvation. Certainly, by the time a girl visibly appears as a woman she should be covered. If an individual comprehends headship teaching and visibly appears as a woman (the symbol of man's glory), she should then be covered. When man's glory appears through natural feminine adolescence, it should disappear during spiritual exercise!

What Constitutes a Head Covering?

With the "why," "when," "who" discussions behind us, let us venture to investigate the "what." The main consideration concerning "what" constitutes an appropriate head covering to be worn by women is the simple biblical meaning of a covering. Since the head covering is to eliminate glories competing with God's, it would seem that the covering should not take on a glory of its own. Any piece of material to cover the head will do. Some contend that the whole face must be veiled, but there is no justification for this as it is the head not the face which is important. Paul instructed the men to remove their head coverings during spiritual exercise. Jewish and Roman men prayed with prayer shawls, or talliths, covering the top, the sides, and the back of the head, but not their faces.

A woman's long hair is given to her for a covering, but the hair does not fully cover her body. Yet, from a heavenly perspective, the woman appears covered – let us not forget the observing angels. The only time that a covering (a veil) is specifically mentioned in the headship text is in verse 15. The Greek word *peribolaion* is used in the phrase *anti peribolaiou* meaning "instead of a veil." *Peribolaion* comes from *peri* – "perimeter" – indicating the natural hair around the head. This refers to the long hair of a woman given her as a covering for her head. Thus, by covering the head, the body is figuratively covered. It stands to reason that the covering used to cover the head about its perimeter (the woman's long hair) should also be concealed by a second covering. This covering should not be so small that the glory of the woman sneaks out from underneath it or so transparent that it peeps through.

What about hats? Dr. Peter J. L. Wee writes:

Hats are also head coverings, but they are subject to dictates of fashion and fancy and may therefore, be extremely colorful, and of various shapes and sizes, and being vanity pieces they may distract worshippers around the wearers. The simplest requirement is a single piece of material, not distracting in color and shape, but one that will help to enhance the atmosphere of worship. These are not stipulations of Scripture but they appear to conform to the requirements of the symbol of the fallen glory of man and woman.[1]

Tertullian writings indicate he was deeply concerned about the adequacy of the head covering:

... because you cannot refuse it, to take some other means to nullify it, by going neither covered nor bare. For some, with their turbans and woolen bands, do not veil their head, but bind it up: protected, indeed, in front, but where the head properly lies, bare. Others are to a certain extent covered over the region of the brain with linen coifs of small dimension.... The region of the veil is (should be) coextensive with the space covered by the hair when unbound: in order that the necks too may be encircled... (who) when about to spend time in prayer itself, with the utmost readiness place a fringe, or a tuft, or any thread whatever, on the crown of their heads, and suppose themselves to be covered? Of so small extent do they falsely imagine their head to be![2]

It was shown in an earlier chapter that the practice of the woman's head covering was degraded by the transition from veils to day bonnets, and finally to fashionable hats in the late 19th century. Perhaps we should learn from past mistakes and not repeat history again. It would seem that any practice which deviates from the simple approach of covering the hair with a mundane piece of cloth is a step away from symbolizing Biblical headship. However, with this said, it may be wise for women to wear a hat during rare occasions so as to not stumble others who do not understand the practice. For example, while visiting a church meeting in which the head covering is not practiced, wearing a hat would be less distracting than a veil. The goal in this situation would be to comply with the scriptural instruction, but in a way that does not cause the ignorant to think evil of you.

In summary, two fundamental guidelines should be used in selecting a proper head covering. First, the head covering used should never take on a glory of its own. In other words, nothing that the woman adorns herself with should call attention to herself (1 Tim. 2:9). Clement of Alexandria summarizes this point bluntly, "Love of display is not for a lady, but a prostitute."[3] Secondly, the head covering selected should accomplish the intended purpose – to conceal the woman's glory (the hair about her head).

Arguments and Defense

The following are popular arguments against the practice of the woman's head covering:

1. Cultural Argument
The head covering practice was an ancient Eastern custom of the day and, therefore, does not apply today.

Defense

Where else in Scripture is the knowledge of ancient Greco-Roman social history a prerequisite to properly interpret Scripture, such that a culturally-based interpretation negates the plain teaching of the passage? Answer: Nowhere. 2 Timothy 3:16 states, *"all Scripture is given by inspiration of God, and is profitable for doctrine, for reproof, for correction, for instruction in righteousness."* When we start undermining divine Scripture with cultural arguments, we begin down a path of human relativity that will erode away the foundation of absolute truth and leave us without any sure footing to stand upon. In this passage, the veil is a mark of subjection to God by the woman. This requirement for subjection to God is not cultural; it is timeless. God knew Christians needed a visible reminder of His authority and order in the church.

William MacDonald writes:

In verses 7-10, Paul teaches the subordination of the woman to the man by going back to creation. This should forever lay to rest any idea that his teaching about women's covering was what was culturally suitable in his day but not applicable to us today. The headship of man and the subjection of woman have been God's order from the beginning.[1]

Dr. H. Wayne House, former professor of Dallas Theological Seminary explains:

Paul bases his view of the relationship between men and women in First Corinthians 11 upon theological considerations from the creation narratives. He is appealing not to social custom but to creation. Paul did not base his teaching on mere opinion of rabbinic bias. He clearly founded his teaching on the creation order.[2]

It is important to remember, as previously shown in this book, that there was not a consistent headdress custom among cultures in Paul's day and that his teaching was contrary to all the cultural practices at that time. Dr. N. J. Gourlay explains this point nicely:

In summary, there was no firm cultural pattern which can be held to have been in agreement with Paul's commands. Given this, it can be shown it is not true, as some would suggest it to be, that the practical application of head covering depends on how far it is understood and recognized in a community.[3]

2. Prostitute Argument
Paul was speaking to only the "converted prostitutes" in the Corinth meeting.

Explanation
The vestal virgins of the temple of Aphrodite were prostitutes and were known to be such because their heads were

shaved and uncovered (supposedly). Therefore, when the women of the Corinthian church had their liberation movement and cast off their coverings, the saved temple prostitutes in the assembly were left completely uncovered (having neither hair nor a veil) and, thus, needed some covering. Therefore, Paul is supposedly asking either the Corinthian women to avoid all appearance of evil by covering their heads all the time in public or he is directing the saved prostitutes to cover their heads until their hair had grown out. In either case, a woman's uncovered head no longer signifies being a prostitute as it once did so the practice is no longer relevant.

Defense

Critics of the head covering practice will often focus their attention on possible social issues of the day, instead of the clear teaching of God's word. One such argument is the prostitution argument just explained. Does Paul introduce the subject of prostitutes at all in 1 Corinthians chapter 11? No, Paul introduces no reference to the social issue of prostitutes in Corinthian society. Neither is there any mention of saved prostitutes among the believers at Corinth or of Paul encouraging the sisters to cover their heads in public as not to look like a prostitute. Besides lacking proof that Paul's writing was influenced by the social ills of prostitutes, the historical evidence suggests that the prostitute theory is flawed at its premise. Lenski describes the historical information:

> As far as prostitutes are concerned, all the evidence that has been discovered proves that only a few of the very lowest types had shorn or shaven heads. As a class these women endeavored to make themselves as attractive as possible and did their utmost to beautify their hair. We cannot, therefore, accept the idea that is advanced by not a few of the best commentators that in our passage Paul refers to the practice of the prostitutes and intends to tell the Corinthian women that, if

they pray or prophesy with uncovered heads, they act the part of a lewd woman.[4]

However, putting the historical evidence and the missing Biblical references to prostitution aside, the fundamental truth of Biblical interpretation is that cultural information is not required to interpret Scripture in such a way that undermines what it clearly states. Paul is addressing divine order and the glories in the assembly. He is addressing "any and every" man and "any and every" woman (the general population of sisters, not the potentially saved prostitutes). The glories and order were not limited to converted temple prostitutes, which may or may not have been in the church meetings. This cultural view would also negate the fact that women have a ministry of teaching angels today. This argument misrepresents the main point of Paul's teaching, which is headship. Headship drives the symbol, not the other way around. Nowhere in 1 Corinthians chapter 11 are women told to wear a veil in order to distinguish themselves from harlots. In fact, their long hair and their dress would distinguish them from temple prostitutes. It is important to remember that Paul only directed women to wear a veil while praying and prophesying, not in everyday life. Certainly, if a woman chose to wear a veil in public, she would not give any impression of being an immoral woman. But, in the local assembly, where the veil was being commanded, everyone would already know if there were converted prostitutes among them; therefore, the argument loses value from a logic perspective.

R. C. Sproul (from Reformed Theological Seminary) states:

Some very subtle means of relativizing the text occur when we read into the text cultural considerations that ought not to be there. For example, with the hair covering issue in Corinth, numerous commentators on the epistle point out that the local sign of the prostitute in Corinth was an uncovered head. Therefore, the argument runs, the reason why Paul wanted women to cover their heads was to avoid a scandalous appearance of Christian women. What is wrong with this kind of speculation? We are not only putting words into Paul's mouth, but ignoring words that are there. Paul provides a rationale which is based on an appeal to creation not the custom of Corinthian harlots. We must be careful not to let our zeal for knowledge of the culture obscure what is actually said. To the subordinate Paul's stated reason to our speculatively conceived reason is to slander the apostle and turn exegesis into eisegesis.[5]

The harlot argument is simply a human explanation of convenience. The holder of this view makes the difference between a believing and an unbelieving woman a matter of mere externals, not of deep spiritual transformation by the Lord and adds a cultural possibility to a divine certainty. Since Paul exhorted a spiritually thriving church to *"abstain from all appearance of evil"* (1 Thess. 5:22), it would seem he would have used even more direct speech in exhorting an assembly full of saved harlots!

3. The Long Hair Argument
The woman's long hair is a natural covering for her so she does not need a veil.

Explanation
1 Corinthians 11:15 indicates that long hair has been given to the woman as an "instead of" covering, meaning that she does not need to wear a veil if she has long hair. The Greek word *anti* translated "for" is different than the standard word normally translated "for." The word *anti*, for example, in 1 Peter 3:9 indicates "in the place of" or "instead of:" *"Not rendering evil **for** evil, or railing **for** railing: but contrariwise blessing; knowing that ye are thereunto called, that ye should inherit a blessing."*

Defense

The word *anti* in verse 15, rendered "for," has a normal meaning of "instead of" or "against," as previously shown. Given the context of 1 Corinthians 11:13-15, *anti* is prompting the reader to compare something with something else in order to answer the question posed in verse 13; "Is it seemly that a woman pray unto God uncovered?" The two things being compared are the long hair of the woman and the short hair of the man, not the long hair of the woman and a veil, which required a "down over the head" action to comply with 1 Corinthians 11:5-6. The man's uncovered head (without long hair) was nature's declaration of his authority over the woman, while the woman's long hair was nature's reminder of her subjection to male leadership and compliance with divine order.

Apparently, the Corinthians were confusing gender roles within the church. Leadership ability or the possessing of a speaking gift does not give one the right to lead or speak in the Church. God's creation order should be visible at all times – symbolic truth would serve as a constant reminder to mankind and the observing angels of God's supreme authority over the Church. Gender distinction and corresponding order was to be highly regarded in the Church.

Long hair is a natural covering with which the woman covers herself; however, a woman's long hair is also a glory to her. Therefore, this glory must also be covered to ensure no other glory except God's (the uncovered man) is seen when Christians gather for spiritual exercise. The Greek words for "cover" or "uncover" in 1 Cor. 11:5, 6, 7, and 13 are formed from the verb *katakalupto* which means "to cover down upon" or literally "to veil." The only remaining reference to a covering is found in v. 15 when Paul is speaking of hair. This is a noun form, *peribolain,* which means "a covering around." There is an action implied. One wears hair. It is fixed; it is not put on and off. If you substitute the word "with hair" or "without hair" for the verb forms of (un)covered in verses 4-5, men must then pray with their heads bald. The substitution makes no sense.

It should be noted that the Greek word group which includes the words translated "cover" and "uncover" in verses 5, 6, 7 and 13, is not used elsewhere in the New Testament to refer to hair, but is used to refer to some other type of covering or veil. However, *katakalupto* is found in the Septuagint (The Greek Old Testament). It is used in Genesis 38:15 to describe the action of Tamar covering her face with a veil according to the previous verse. *Katakalupto* is also found in Esther 6:12 to describe Haman's action of covering his head while he hurried home. It is obvious that Haman did not instantly grow long hair to show his shame, but had thrown a covering over his head. *Akatakaluptos*, found in 1 Cor. 11:5 and 13 describes the act of uncovering. This word is also found once in the Septuagint, but no where else in the New Testament other than 1 Corinthians 11. In Leviticus 13:45, a man declared by the priest to be a leper was to "uncover" his head (to be bareheaded) – he could not hide his condition from others. Clearly, this passage indicates that the application of *akatakaluptos* is to uncover the head, not to cut one's hair off.

It is concluded that neither the context of the 1 Corinthians 11 passage or the literal meaning of the Greek verbs employed in the passage are used elsewhere in Scripture to describe the act of wearing long hair or cutting hair. Obviously, the action described is covering down over something. By implication, this would mean a woman was to cover her head with a detachable object such as cloth and a man should remove any detachable covering from his head. It is regrettable that the New International Version of the Bible has incorrectly interpreted and noted the action of covering and uncovering as the wearing or not wearing of long hair.

4. A Scriptural Principle without Symbolic Relativity

The head covering is symbolic of submission; therefore, I fulfill the obligation of the symbol by being obedient to male authority as unto God; thus, no covering is required.

<u>Defense</u>

This argument acknowledges scriptural principle, but not symbolic relativity. Some use the same argument to refrain from the Lord's Supper. They say: "I believe in Christ and have appropriated His body and His blood to my life. I don't need to look at the symbols anymore." The Christian must not forget that these symbols were given to "remind" the church of spiritually significant truths that God does not want us to forget.

We humans need persistent visual reminders of God's grace and love lest our affections grow cold and our hearts become calloused. These reminders must be God-originated to prevent humanly derived ideologies and traditions from becoming idols in our midst. God has given three practices of symbolic truth to the church. These serve to refresh our memories about specific truths that God does not want us to forget. The Lord's Supper, where bread and wine are required, was given to remind us of the Lord's broken body and His shed blood, which bought the believer's redemption. Believer's baptism was also instituted. Here water is required to demonstrate the positional truth of dying and being raised up anew in Christ. And lastly, headship was declared. For this truth, a covering of some type is required to demonstrate divine order. Only three simple practices; yet much of Christendom is neglecting or perverting the plain teaching of these or adding their own religious devices. In a real way, the veil preserves our awareness of a permanently existing divine arrangement. When a woman wears a covering and a man removes his cap, it is a token to God that they have accepted His rule and designated plan for ordering our lives.

Mary Kassian, the author of "Women, Creation and the Fall," states, "Since the seventies a myriad of books and articles have been published on the biblical role of women. Yet much confusion remains. I have found the bulk of writing on the biblical role of the women irresponsible in the their handling of the Bible."[6] She also writes concerning the action of the Corinthian women removing their head coverings: "The discarding of this symbol went far beyond mere cosmetic adjustment. It was an affront to the order God had instituted at creation."[7]

The argument to hand wave symbolic truth from the 1 Corinthian passage centers on what the word "head" actually means. Does it mean "authority" or literally "the head?" Actually, both meanings are implied in the 1 Corinthian 11; the subject of *headship* is a key theme. In verse 3 "head" speaks of authority, in verse 4 and 5 both meanings are implied (dishonoring one's spiritual head via covering or uncovering the physical head). Verse 6 necessitates a physical head meaning. Verse 7 explains why there is a need for symbolic representation of headship (men and woman represent two icons which have related glories). In verse 7, it is obvious that the physical heads of men and women are in view. The man is not to be covered – he represents God, and thus reflects God's glory in creation (Heb. 2:7-9). The covered heads of women and uncovered heads of men were to be a constant *visible* reminder of headship – God's creation order among the genders and to Himself.

5. No Such Custom Argument
Doesn't 1 Corinthians 11:16 state that there was no such custom of wearing the head covering?

Defense
It is agreed that the Greek construction of this verse causes the meaning to be difficult to ascertain. However, it would be illogical to think that Paul wrote 13 verses addressing the importance of the head covering only for him to contradict himself in v. 16. Given the clear context of the head covering passage and

the epistle as a whole, verse 16 should be interpreted in light of the obvious discussion and the need of order in the assembly. Besides a logical contextual defense, the historical documentation (see earlier chapters) declares that most women did cover themselves in public.

Matthew Henry writes concerning verse 16:

> He [Paul] sums up all by referring those who were contentious to the usages and customs of the churches in v. 16. Custom is in a great measure the rule of decency. And the common practice of the churches is what he would have them govern themselves by. He does not silence the contentious by mere authority, but lets them know that they would appear to the world as very odd and singular in their humor if they would quarrel for a custom to which all the churches of Christ were at that time utter strangers, or against a custom in which they all concurred, and that upon the ground of natural decency. It was the common usage of the churches for women to appear in public assemblies, and join in public worship, veiled; and it was manifestly decent that they should do so.[8]

6. Counter Argument Teaching Style

Paul uses an argument in vv. 3-10 that serves as a building block to support the final counter argument in vv. 11-15 – that the woman's hair is the covering instead of the veil.

Defense

Paul never states that this is his mode of teaching. Paul does occasionally use the objector/defender teaching style in some of his epistles, but usually to support a final conclusion, which he has already thoroughly addressed. One of his longest indulgences is in Romans 3:1-8. For two chapters, he has used logic and Old Testament Scripture to conclude that all men are sinners and deserve divine judgment. The point/counterpoint verbiage in

vv. 1-8 of chapter 3 is the finale of his conclusion. It is the frosting on the cake of his argument of God's holiness and man's depravity. There is also no more than one verse for point, and not many verses for counterpoints, as some would state is the case in 1 Corinthians 11.

7. The Wife vs Woman Argument
Paul is speaking only to wives and not all the sisters.

Explanation
The passage must refer to married women only, as only married sisters are to be subject to their own husbands. Unmarried sisters, therefore, need not wear head coverings.

Defense
It is argued, and rightfully so, that all women are not to be in subjection to all men. This would be an abhorrent and appalling interpretation of the passage and one that does not agree with the rest of Scripture. "Wives submit yourselves unto your *own* husbands" (Col. 3:18), and "Wives, submit yourselves unto your *own* husbands, as unto the Lord" (Eph. 5:22). If the wearing of a head covering implies that all women are in subjection to all men, young and old, married and unmarried, women will understandably not want to do it. However, this is not what Paul is teaching. What he is addressing is the principle of male authority and female subjugation in God-appointed relationships of all authority. The head covering is symbolizing this overall order and not a specific authority which may relate to a woman such as her husband, father, elders, etc.

8. The Women Speaking Argument
Paul is teaching in 1 Cor. 11:5 that only those women who lead the assembly in prayer and publicly teach must have their heads covered.

Defense

This view is inference only.

Dr. John Robbins writes:
By here condemning the one (speaking with uncovered head) he does not commend the other (speaking). If one were to say, it is wrong to speed through a red light, he cannot be understood to say that it is right to speed. It is wrong both to speed and to ignore red lights. So it is with women speaking in church uncovered. Women speaking uncovered in church is wrong, and so is women speaking in church.[9]

Paul's subject matter is spiritual headship and not speaking roles, which he addresses in great detail three chapters later in chapter 14. The word "head" occurs eight times, and the word "cover" or a derivative occurs seven times in the 1 Cor. 11:2-16 text. In contrast, praying is mentioned three times and prophesying only twice.

Robert Billings, Jr. writes:

Explicitly the verse says that a woman who prays or prophesies with her head uncovered dishonors her head. There is no explicit sanctioning of women speaking with their heads covered. The inference that women may speak with their heads covered contradicts Paul's explicit command in 1 Cor. 14:34-35 not to speak in the church meeting. Since the Christian should submit to the clear commands in Scripture, the teaching of 1 Cor. 14:34-35 should be followed.[10]

Were women speaking in the Corinthian church meetings? Given the sharp warning of 1 Corinthians 11:5 and the prohibition of women speaking in the church (1 Cor. 14:34), we may assume so, else why would Paul write so emphatically. The flavor of the passage is to reign in what was not appropriate, rather than to endorse an activity that other portions of Scripture forbid – truth is found in the whole of God's Word.

9. The passive Greek verbs used in verses 5-7 indicate that there is no action demanded by men or women concerning the covering and uncovering of their heads.

Defense

It is noted that the Greek present tense spelling is the same for both the passive and the middle voice, except for present participles. Most Analytical Greek Lexicons do not identify the middle voice option for these present tense verbs. Consequently, one must rely upon the context of a passage to determine if the form should be translated as passive (the subject being acted upon) or middle (the subject acting on itself or in its own interest). The middle voice brings the connotation of a deliberate action taken by a person on themselves or in their own interest. For example, the present active indicative may be translated as "I cover my head." The middle voice active indicative would be translated "I cover my own head." Because of the clear context of the passage, Ken Wuest's Expanded Translations of the New Testament renders the passive/middle voice verbs in I Corinthians 11:5-7 as middle voice and not as passive voice:

> *But every woman while praying or prophesying with her head uncovered dishonors her head, for this would be one and the same thing as if she had her head shaved. For, assuming that a woman is uncovered, let her also cut her hair close. But since it is dishonorable for a woman to be shaven or have her hair cropped close, let her put a shawl down over her head* (1 Cor. 1:5-6).[11]

The three verbs in question, with their associated tense, mood, and voice information are listed below:

Verse 6: "not covered" – indicative present middle
Verse 6: "be covered" – imperative present middle
Verse 7: "not to cover" – infinitive present middle

The first occurrence of the verb κατακαλυπτω in verse 6 implies a continuing statement of fact: "if she does not cover her own head, it is a shame to her; she might as well have her head shorn."

The second occurrence of κατακαλυπτω in verse 6 implies an ongoing command: "if it be a shame to a woman to be shorn or shaven, she should cover herself." There is action implied because it is translated as middle voice – the woman covers herself.

The condition and timing of the continual action is defined by the participles in verse 5 – praying or prophesying. To denote that the action indicated by the participles accompanies the action indicated by the following verbs, these participles may be translated using the phrase "while praying or prophesying." Thus, praying and prophesying define when the woman is to have her head covered or the man to have his head uncovered.

The verb in verse 7 is a verbal noun in the middle voice to convey continuous action: "of the man to maintain no covering on his head during times of prayer and teaching." The uncovered head is the act of a man acting upon himself. This seems to relate a deliberate action taken by the man to be sure his head is not covered while praying or prophesying.

Logically, let us consider the two options of covering: hair or an external piece of cloth. Hair as a covering will be considered first. Does the act of covering or not covering in verses 4-6 refer to men not maintaining hair on their heads or not growing hair on their heads, and that women are to maintain hair on their heads or are to continue growing hair on their heads? The present infinitive in verse 7 indicates that the man must either "repeatedly" not have his head covered with hair or not "continuously" grow hair. It is obvious that the action is not "growing hair" for both men and women grow hair during the church meetings. Nor can the subject be growing long hair because women would never be able to cut it and men can't stop growing hair. Logically speaking, if the "down over covering" in verses 5-6 is hair, as some assert, then men would have to be bald and stop growing hair.

If a passive voice understanding were applied to the "down over covering," the women should always be covered, and men can never be uncovered. The middle voice interpretation is the only logical conclusion: "men and women are to act upon themselves (their heads) or their own interest by covering/uncovering their heads" – the act of "covering down over" must actively involve an external covering.

To summarize, only an external covering with a middle voice understanding can satisfy the language of an ongoing action of men and women covering and uncovering while praying or prophesying, as it would be impossible to be covered and uncovered continuously (with either hair or a veil). Only an external covering satisfies the explanation of women being as shorn or having her hair cut short if not covered. Only an external covering satisfies the language of men praying uncovered, not speaking of being bald – a fixed non-covering. Men and women are to act upon themselves (their heads) or in their own interest by covering/uncovering their heads.

10. **I understand that the woman is the glory of the man, but it seems strange that the woman's natural covering (her long hair) would be considered a glory. If there are no other scriptural examples of a covering being a glory in itself, why then should the woman's hair be considered a glory that must be covered during times of praying and prophesying.**

Defense

The pattern of Scripture is consistent in both identifying coverings which pose a glory in themselves and when such coverings should be seen or not seen depending upon whether the glory each represents should be revealed or concealed. Please consider the following examples (this is not an exhaustive list):

Ex. 28:40   *"And for Aaron's sons thou shalt make coats, and thou shalt make for them girdles, and bonnets shalt thou make for them, for glory and for beauty."* Remember, the gold plate upon the miter was a replacement glory of God, since the man was covered.

Ex. 29:43   *"And there I will meet with the children of Israel, and the tabernacle shall be sanctified by My glory."* The Tabernacle (a huge covering – tent) was a reflection of God's glory.

Num. 16:42   *"And it came to pass, when the congregation was gathered against Moses and against Aaron, that they looked toward the tabernacle of the congregation: and, behold, the cloud covered it, and the glory of the Lord appeared."* The cloud that covered the Tabernacle radiated the glory of the Lord for all to see. A similar sight was noticed at the transfiguration of the Lord Jesus Christ. The Father, while speaking of His Son, was concealed by a cloud, yet brilliantly shined forth His glory (the cloud concealed God's full glory, but still reflected His glory for man to see).

1 Kings 8:11   *"So that the priests could not stand to minister because of the cloud: for the glory of the Lord had filled the house of the Lord."* A covering cloud concealed God's full glory yet reflected His glory to mankind – even the reflected glory overwhelmed mortal men.

Ps. 19:1   *"The heavens declare the glory of God; and the fir-mament sheweth His handywork."* The very firma-ments that cover the earth display the glory of God.

Prov. 16:31   *"The hoary head is a crown of glory, if it be found in the way of righteousness."* The gray hair that nor-mally covers the elderly displays the glory of their wisdom gained through experience.

Matt. 6:29-30 *"And yet I say unto you, That even Solomon in all his glory was not arrayed like one of these. Wherefore, if God so clothe [cover] the grass of the field, which to day is, and to morrow is cast into the oven, shall He not much more clothe you, O ye of little faith?"*

1 Peter 5:4   *"And when the chief Shepherd shall appear, ye shall receive a crown of glory that fadeth not away."* Those who shepherd God's sheep well will be re-warded with a crown (to cover the head), which dis-plays the glory of the Chief Shepherd.

Rev. 19:8   *"And to her [the bride of Christ] was granted that she should be arrayed in fine linen, clean and white; for the fine linen is the righteousness of saints."* Christ pleaded with the church of Laodicea to have *"white raiment, that thou mayest be clothed, and that the shame of thy nakedness do not appear"* (Rev. 3:18).

Since all true believers have already received the im-puted righteousness of Christ (justification occurs at regeneration), the reference to white garments by our Lord is speaking of the righteous acts of the saints, that which is done with pure motive and in the strength and power of the Holy Spirit. These right-eous acts are rewardable by Christ and serve to en-hance the believer with a spiritual brilliance of the Savior that will never diminish. Rewards earned during our sojourn on earth have direct bearing on our appreciation for heaven and capacity to worship God forever. In the resurrection, some saints will shine brighter than others (1 Cor. 15:41-42) for what is done in this life for Christ provides a reflective covering of glory in heaven. Glory is a thing of degrees; glory has a distinct weight to it. *"For our light affliction, which is but for a moment, worketh for us a far more exceeding and eternal weight of glory"* (2 Cor. 4:17).

The tabernacle concealing God's personal presence, the gray hair covering the heads of the elderly, the lilies covering the earth, the long hair on women, the clouds that both obscured and reflected God's glory, and the priestly garments are all examples of glorious coverings. We conclude that coverings throughout the Bible are used to either conceal a particular glory or reveal a reflective glory of God. The covering is not something to be disdained, but to be appreciated for the ministry that it performs in upholding the glory of God.

To God Be the Glory

The glory of God is witnessed in creation, in the regeneration of lost souls, and in miracles which confound the laws of science and human reasoning; therefore, His glory illuminates each and every page of Scripture. God's glory serves as a beacon for all humanity to consider who He is, rather than just what He does. To this end, Scripture supplies man with incredible insight into the character and attributes of God, thus, ensuring our respect and reverence. The outshining of God's essence beckons us to consider our own frail existence and our accountability *to Him with whom we have to do.* His glory is paramount in all things, in all places and for all time and eternity.

Those who reject the teaching that the symbolic practice of the head covering affirms God's glory by covering competing glories may argue: "Who says that God limits other glories from being revealed in His presence?" "And if competing glories are allowed in heaven, then certainly the unveiled woman is acceptable in the church gatherings which meet in the Lord's presence on earth." In the realm of spiritual matters, human objection and rejection is silenced by God's infallible and immutable Word. So what does God's Word declare about divine glory, rival glories, and how coverings reveal God's glory and conceal competing glories?

First, let us consider the question, "Should all glories other than God's direct outshining intrinsic glory be concealed in His presence as to ensure no other glories are seen?" The answer is "yes," if what is visible is a *competing glory* and "no," if what is seen is a *reflective glory*. Before defending this conclusion, may we ponder together certain timeless realities pertaining to God's glory:

Ps. 57:5:   *Be thou exalted, O God, above the heavens;* ***let Thy glory be above all the earth***.

Ps. 96:7-8:   *Give unto the Lord, O ye kindreds of the people, give unto the Lord glory and strength.* ***Give unto the Lord the glory*** *due unto His name: bring an offering, and come into His courts.*

Ps. 115:1:   *Not unto us, O Lord, not unto us, but unto Thy name* ***give glory***, *for Thy mercy, and for Thy truth's sake.*

Isa. 42:8:   *I am the Lord: that is My name: and* ***My glory will I not give to another***, *neither My praise to graven images.*

Isa. 43:7:   *Even every one that is called by My name: for* ***I have created him for My glory***, *I have formed him; yea, I have made him.*

Isa. 48:11:   *For Mine own sake, even for Mine own sake, will I do it: for how should My name be polluted? and* ***I will not give My glory unto another***.

Gal. 6:14:   *But* ***God forbid that I should glory, save in the cross of our Lord Jesus Christ***, *by whom the world is crucified to me, and I unto the world.*

1 Cor. 10:31: *Whether therefore ye eat, or drink, or* ***whatsoever ye do, do all to the glory of God***.

2 Cor 10:17: *But* ***he that glorieth, let him glory in the Lord***.

It is concluded that man's highest occupation is to glorify God and that God does not permit others to intrude upon His supreme position and authority or to diminish His outshining glory. C. S. Lewis colorfully asserts the later point: "A man can no more diminish God's glory by refusing to worship Him than a lunatic can put out the sun by scribbling the word *darkness* on the walls of his cell."[1]

All glory is to be God's, and all glorying is to be directed towards God. The believer, by the Holy Spirit, is capable of manifesting God's glory for others to see because he or she is one with God in Christ (John 17:22). God is the source of divine glory, but through creation He has designed means of *reflecting* His glory back to Himself and of *concealing* competing glories (both actions provide created beings an opportunity to worship God)!

This reflecting and concealing reality is characteristic of all that we appreciate in Christ. For example, let us consider God's love (His sacrificial giving in action) for a moment. *God is love* – He is the source of all true love (1 Jn. 4:8). God extended His love to mankind by the giving of His own Son as a substitutionary sacrifice (He sourced love to us through Christ – 1 Jn. 4:9-10). The result is twofold: First, *"We love Him* [God], *because He first loved us"* (1 Jn. 4:19) and secondly, *"Beloved, let us love one another: for love is of God; and every one that loveth is born of God, and knoweth God"* (1 Jn. 4:7).

God's love was not sourced to us to be absorbed and hoarded, it is to be directed back to God in heart-felt appreciation and devotion or to be reflected to others that they might witness God's love in action and then direct praise back to God also. Likewise, Christians are not to outwardly manifest the self-centered nature of their own flesh, or allegiance to a corrupt world system (these are competing with God's perfect love and order). All of what God bestows to us is for the purpose of reflecting admiration back to Him or to cause others to do the same.

Reflected Glories

In the beginning, all creation perfectly displayed the glory of God. Even after *"creation was subjected to futility"* (Rom. 8:20; NKJV) by human rebellion and the subsequent curses of God, Paul states, *"For the invisible things of Him from the creation of the world are clearly seen, being understood by the things that are made, even His eternal power and Godhead, so that they [men] are without excuse"* (Rom. 1:20). Even though tainted and damaged by sin, creation still furnishes overwhelming evidence of a Master-designer; creation demands a Creator. Celestial and terrestrial bodies continue to reflect God's glory and cause mortal men everywhere to gaze heavenward and ponder the vastness of God (1 Cor. 15:40).

Beyond the observable creation is the invisible domain of spiritual beings. In describing the outshining glory of God and the spectacular nature of His throne, the Holy Spirit referred to angelic beings for the purpose of better accentuating specific aspects of God's splendor (Isa. 6 and Rev. 4). As we read these accounts, our focus is not to be drawn to the creatures themselves, but into a fuller appreciation of Christ through what is symbolically displayed by their visage. Just as a mirror reflects the light received from an object back to an observer, these spiritual beings, through Scripture, are reflecting the moral and essential glories of Christ. We are to adore and rejoice in what is seen (the glory of God). We are not to revere what is covered (competing glories which would distract from Christ) or the means itself used to reflect God's glory (i. e. spiritual beings).

For example: The Four Living Creatures cry out *"Holy, Holy, Holy Lord God Almighty, which was, and is, and is to come"* (Rev. 4:8). The importance of the text is not to show that these creatures can verbalize praise, but that God is separate from and above all creation. Where their features are described it is not to bring glory to themselves, but to reflect the glory of Christ:

v. 6: Full of eyes (before and behind) represents God's eternal omniscience (also seen in Christ, Rev. 5:6 – seven eyes).

v. 7: The faces of these beings are uncovered because each face represents a distinct vantage point in which the Lord Jesus is displayed in the Gospel accounts. The lion's face reflects Matthew's presentation of Christ as the rightful heir to the throne of David; He is the Jewish King – the lion is king of the beasts. The face of the Ox (a beast of burden) represents Mark's humble servant perspective of Christ. The human face portrays Christ's humanity as shown in the Gospel according to Luke. John affords us the heavenly view of Christ's deity as symbolized by the eagle (who is able to soar high above the earth).

v. 8: Six wings, though not specifically stated here, both Cherubim and Seraphim cover certain parts of themselves with these wings while in God's presence (Isa. 6, Ezek. 1); therefore, it is likely that the Four Living Creatures do also – these creatures may be actual Seraphim. Where their feet and heads are described as replacement glories or symbols of God's glory, they remain uncovered. When, for example, their feet are not needed to reflect a glory of Christ, each is covered and not described.

v. 9: They declare the glory of God not only visibly, but audibly. They give God glory, honor and thanks.

In every aspect that is described to us, the Four Living Creatures reflect the glory of Christ. The same symbolic representation of Christ is seen in the description of the Cherubim in Ezekiel chapter 1. However, the faces of the Seraphim, as described in Isaiah chapter 6, are not described to us. Why is this? Because their faces are hidden (no visible reflected glory of Christ is portrayed in this scene). What is covered is not described – it is not what the Holy Spirit wants us to be occupied with. There is no description of the Seraph's wings, except in number, which provides essential information to their ministry (they fly above the throne of God, and they conceal their own intrinsic glory). Their wings are mentioned to highlight their use in God-ordained ministry, not to emphasize their aerodynamic abilities. The specific language ensures all glory is of and to God.

Understanding the symbolic significance of each of the revealed portions of these spiritual beings is integral to better appreciating the fuller glory of God; else why would the Holy Spirit have purposefully provided the extra revelation. The importance of the symbolic ministry provided by the Four Living Creatures, Seraphim, and Cherubim before the throne of God has been acknowledged by many theologians.

Matthew Henry: [Why do the Seraphim cover themselves in God's presence?] "This bespeaks their great humility and reverence in their attendance upon God, for He is greatly feared." "… in the presence of God, they cover … because, being conscious of an infinite distance from the divine perfections, they are ashamed to show their faces."[2]

Albert Barnes: [Why do the Seraphim cover their faces?] "This is designed, doubtless, to denote the reverence and awe inspired by the immediate presence of God." "The seraphim stood covered, or as if concealing themselves as much as possible, in token of their nothingness and unworthiness in the presence of the Holy One."[3]

William MacDonald: "The creatures symbolize those attributes of God which are seen in creation: His majesty, power, swiftness, and wisdom." Of the Seraphim he writes, "with four wings for reverence and two for service. These celebrate the holiness of God."[4]

Warren Wiersbe: "These creatures [Seraphim] symbolize the glory and power of God."[5] "These creatures [the Four Living Creatures] signify the wisdom of God (full of eyes) and proclaim the holiness of God."[6]

P. P. Enns: "*Cherubim* are … created with indescribable powers and beauty …. Their main purpose and activity might be summarized in this way: they are proclaimers and protectors of God's glorious presence, His sovereignty, and His holiness."[7]

Adam Clarke: "And the living creatures stand before the throne of glory; and they stand in fear, in trembling, in horror, and in great agitation; and from this agitation a stream of fire flows before them. Of the two seraphim one stands at the right hand of the holy blessed God, and one stands at the left; and each has six wings: with two they cover their face lest they should see the face of the shechinah; with two they cover their feet lest they should find out the footstool of the shechinah; and with two they fly, and sanctify his great name. And they answer each other, saying Holy, holy, holy, Lord God of hosts; the whole earth is full of his glory. And the living creatures stand near his glory, yet they do not know the place of his glory; but wheresoever his glory is, they cry out and say, Blessed be the glory of the Lord in his place."[8]

Coverings That Conceal and Reveal Glories

Coverings throughout the Old Testament are used to show that God is holy, separate from sin and sinners, and that man cannot approach Him. The tabernacle with all its internal and external coverings serves as a great example. Coverings are consistently used to show submission to authority throughout Scripture. Rebekah immediately covered her head with a veil after learning that her espoused husband Isaac was approaching from the field (Gen. 24:65); in doing so, she was symbolically affirming his authority over her.

Ashes above the lip, sackcloth on the body, and dirt on the head are used throughout the Old Testament to show humility, submission and lowliness. Where one symbol representing God's glory is not apparent it is replaced with another. As explained earlier, the High Priest wore a miter, but upon the miter there was a gold front piece which represented God's perfection and purity. When the priest covered his head with the miter, a substitute symbol of God's glory was displayed (in this case, gold was used in place of the man to represent the glory of God).

The cherubim above the mercy seat in the Tabernacle were not covering the mercy seat, otherwise how would it be possible for the High Priest to sprinkle blood upon it? Rather the cherubim were overshadowing it – shielding the glory of God from penetrating outward and, at the same time, covering themselves. While inhabiting with His people, the nation of Israel, He dwelled above the mercy seat and between the cherubim (Ex. 25:22; 37:9). Why was Moses able to stand before God in the holy place and not be consumed? Why could God speak to Moses *face to face, as a man speaketh unto his friend?* Because the Cherubim were protecting Moses from God's radiant glory. God Himself discloses this fact in responding to Moses' request to gaze upon Him. The Lord told Moses that he would not live if He granted such a request, but God did present Moses with an alternative: *"And it shall come to pass, while My glory passeth by, that I will put thee in a clift of the rock, and will cover thee with My hand while I pass by"* (Ex. 33:22). Moses could not view God's *Shekinah* and live, but he was permitted to appreciate what he was able – God's *after-glow.*

There is a significant difference between the full manifestation of God's glory and His omnipresence. Revelation Chapters 4 and 5 shows us that all three persons of the Godhead are visibly in the throne room of heaven, yet each is still omnipresent.

We don't read of the angels covering themselves with wings while accompanying the Lord to visit Abraham. Why? Because the Lord and angels were veiled in human form (in the same way that Hebrews 10:20 speaks of the Lord's flesh being a veil of His essential glory). Additionally, the cherubim guarding the entrance to the Garden of Eden are not spoken of as covering themselves. In fact, I can find no example in Scripture in which the angel's wings are mentioned except when they are in the intimate unshielded presence of God's glory. The angels that visited Abraham in Genesis chapter 18 didn't need wings for covering (nor for flying for that matter) because they were temporarily veiled in human flesh.

What do you think would happen if one of the covering cherubs, while in God's presence, decided to brashly extend all four of its wings up in the air to reveal its inherent beauty rather than to fulfill its appointed covering ministry? Apparently, this sin was committed by *a covering cherub* named Lucifer long ago (Isa. 14:12-15; Ezek. 28:12-17). The actual scene is not recorded for us to know, but given his self-exalting speech and his God-given ministry, there can be little doubt that Lucifer wanted to be seen and to be appreciated in heaven the same way God was – for he sought to display his glory and to ascend to the throne of God. God responded by condemning Lucifer, *"Thine heart was **lifted up because of thy beauty**; thou hast corrupted thy wisdom by **reason of thy brightness**; I will cast thee to the ground"* (Ezek. 28:17). Competing glories and flaunting outward beauty while gathered in the Lord's presence cannot be tolerated – let the Church take note!

Where in all of Scripture do we see any other glory present when God's glory is clearly displayed? Should the Church engage in such an offensive behavior while gathered in the name of Christ? We have lost sight of the glory of God and our God-given *revealing* and *concealing* ministry to manifest the glory of Christ to all that is seen and unseen: *"To the intent that now, unto the principalities and powers in heavenly places, might be* known by the Church the manifold wisdom of God, according to the eternal purpose which He purposed in Christ Jesus our Lord" (Eph. 3:10-11). **"To God be the Glory, great things He hath done!"**

Conclusion

In Paul's pursuit to restore order in the Corinth church, he gives five reasons for men to be bareheaded and for women to cover their heads during spiritual exercise (1 Cor. 11:2-16).

1. **To show agreement with divine order and headship.** *"For this cause ought the woman to have [a sign of authority] on her head"* (v. 10). The veil is a symbol of submission to God's authority; when worn, the woman shows visible agreement with divine order (verse 3).

2. **To ensure God's glory is seen and competing glories are concealed.** The man is God's representative (God's glory) and is to remain uncovered. However, the woman, representing man's glory, is to be covered. Long hair is a fitting covering for the woman, but this covering also is a glory in itself (v. 15), which must be covered so as to not compete with God's glory. When the brothers remain uncovered and the sisters cover during church meetings, all competing glories are thus concealed and only God's glory is seen. This mimics the scene around the throne of God in heaven, where the heavenly creatures also conceal their own intrinsic glories by the use of their own wings, so that only God's glory can be seen.

3. **The angels are watching and learning about submission and order (v. 10, 1 Pet. 1:12).** Paul states that God is using

the Church to teach the angels about subjection and His grace (Eph. 3:10).

4. **Nature itself teaches the significance of the glories.** The human conscience reflected in the vast cultures of the world demonstrates that the woman is to have long hair and the man is to have shorter hair. Why? God teaches from nature that a covering should conceal the woman and, thus, reveal the authority of the man over her. In this way, adherence to God's order is visually apparent.

5. **The Corinthian Church was unusual from other church gatherings**. The implication from verse 16 is that if the Corinthians did not abide by the head covering practice their assembly would be unusual from other church gatherings.

The head covering practice is deeply rooted in God's unchanging headship order. History has testified that for nearly two millennia the church faithfully submitted to Scripture and visually displayed this order symbolically by the head covering practice. Today, just as they did two thousand years ago, the sisters should veil their heads, and the brothers should remove their hats. This applies for any corporate or informal meeting where Christians are occupied with prayer, teaching and worship. An individual's conscience should rule the practice for private prayer.

Dr. Peter J. L. Wee writes concerning the seriousness of the head covering practice:

> The importance of the head covering and the seriousness of its observance by every believer in assembly gatherings can be gauged from the great doctrines that Paul brings to bear upon the teaching. The practice is linked with, and is an expression of, the following doctrines: the authority of the Lord, the authority of His Word, revelation by the Lord, inspiration of the Holy Spirit, headship and its implications with regard to salva-

tion, subordination and submission to the Lord, the glory of God, the glory of man, the glory of woman, the fact of creation, equality and interdependence of man and woman, angels, and the believer's response of obedience to the Lord's commands. Head covering practice is the simplest demonstration and minimal external evidence and expression of a believer's willingness in the realm of submission and obedience to the Lord Jesus Christ. It should be observed with joy and gratitude.[1]

Watchman Nee was a martyr for Christ. He died in 1972 after being in a Chinese labor camp for twenty years. He explains why the head covering is a sign of submitting to God's authority:

Today woman has a sign of authority on her head because of the angels, that is, as a testimony to the angels. Only the sisters in the church can testify to this, for the women of the world know nothing of it. Today when the sisters have the sign of authority on their heads, they bear the testimony that, "I have covered my head so that I do not have my own head, for I do not seek to be head. My head is veiled, and I have accepted man as head, and to accept man as head means that I have accepted Christ as head and God as head. But some of you angels have rebelled against God." This is what it meant "because of the angels."

I have on my head a sign of authority. I am a woman with my head covered. This is a most excellent testimony to the angels, to the fallen and to the unfallen ones. No wonder Satan persistently opposes the matter of head covering. It really puts him to shame. We are doing what he has failed to do. What God did not receive from the angels, He now has from the church.[2]

Everyone should understand that the head covering is not a requirement for salvation – that is through trusting in the finished work of Christ alone! The head covering is not a ritual through which some special blessing is obtained. Wearing a

139

head covering is not proof of spirituality or godly superiority. It seems strange that a modest piece of cloth should be disdained by so many today. But sadder yet is the fact that this token of humble submission should become a catalyst for stubbornness and rebellion among believers. What spirit is this? It certainly is not the Lord's.

In some respects, the biblical teaching of the New Testament regarding the woman's role is difficult to understand and accept amid the current cultural ideals and trends in our society. The God of the Bible is not interested in oppressing women. History has shown that it was Christianity that elevated women to their rightful equality with men. Yet this equality has a prescribed social order, which God established at the time of creation. Contrary to modern thinking, a woman is truly liberated and gains a sense of being fulfilled when she willingly submits to God's unique design for her. If you're not experiencing the joy of being a liberated woman, perhaps a visual reminder of God's authority in your life will aid your quest for contentment. For one's significance and security is only found in the Lord Jesus!

Commenting on obedience to Biblical Christian practices, Charles Finney once proclaimed, "You will appear eccentric. Your obedience will challenge others." Our society is bulging with self-seeking, and self-promoting people that need to be challenged to consider submitting to God. In a culture which loathes meekness and submission to authority, it requires spiritual strength and sheer bravery for a sister to cover herself in public. Perhaps for those sisters who are persecuted for their convictions the veil itself becomes a badge of courage for all to witness! Be of good cheer – the Lord is pleased. Remember He did not entrust the visual beauty of the local assembly to the brothers, but to the sisters. Sisters, you're on display for the entire universe to see. The angels are watching you. Will you be a glory seen or unseen?

Appendix A

Women Depicted Veiled
In Various 3rd and 4th Century
Catacomb Artwork

Veiled Woman
Catacomb of Priscilla (220 A.D.)

Veiled Woman
Coemeterium Maius (late 3rd Century)

Veiled Woman
Crypt of the Saints (late 3rd Century)

Tomb of Two Women
Catacomb of Thraso

Veiled Women
Catacomb of Jordani (4th Century)

Pictures from Torch Publications, Eureka, MT,
"The Veil in Early Christian Art" by Tom Shank

Endnotes

Introduction
1. William Kelly, *Introduction Lectures New Testament Volume II – Paul's Epistles*; (Believers Bookshelf, Sunbury, PA; 1970), pp. 76-77

What is Symbolic Truth?
1. John Chrysostom, *Homily XXVI:2 – On the Veiling of Women*; cited in The Nicene and Post-Nicene Fathers, (Philip Schaff, ed., Grand Rapids, MI: Eerdmans Publishing Co).

Let Church History Speak
1. David Bercot, *A Dictionary of Early Christian Beliefs* – Veil, (Hendrickson Publishers, Peabody, Mass.; 1998), p. 666
2. Irenaeus, *Against Heresies*, Book 1, 8:2, cited in The Ante-Nicene Fathers, A. Cleveland Cox, ed., (The Christian Literature Publishing Co., 1885), I:327.
3. Clement of Alexandria, *The Instructor*, Book 3, (T & T Clark, Edinburgh Scotland; 1989), p. 290
4. David Bercot, op. cit., p. 666
5. Tertullian, On the Veiling of Virgins, translated by David W. Bercot, (Scroll Publishing, Tyler, TX; 1991), p.139
6. David Bercot, op. cit., p. 667
7. Hippolytus, A. Cleveland Cox, ed. cited in The Ante-Nicene Fathers, (The Christian Literature Publishing Co.; 1885), V:257
8. John Chrysostom, op. cit., XIII:149
9. Dwight Strubhar, *Can History Speak*, (Torch Publications, Eureka, MT; 1988), Chapter 4
10. David Bercot, op. cit., p. 668
11. Philip Schaff, ed., Jerome, Letter CXLVII:5, op. cit., VI:292
12. Augustine, *To Possidius, the Elder*, Letters of Augustine #238, (T & T Clark, Edinburgh Scotland; 1989), p. 588
13. Philip Schaff, ed., Augustine, op. cit., vol. 3, 523
14. Angelcynn, *Clothing and Appearance of the Early Christian Anglo-Saxons* (reference 600-800 AD).

145

Let Church History Speak (cont.)

15. Madeleine Ginsburg, *The Hat: Trends and Traditions*, (Barrons Educational Series; 1990)
16. Susan Carroll-Clark from website sclark@epas.utoroto.ca
17. Carolyn Priest-Dorman, *Mistress Thora Sharptooth, OL, Viking Women's Garb in Art and Archaeology.*
18. John Knox, *First Blast of the Trumpet Against the Monstrous Regiment of Women*, David Lang, ed. Vol. 4, p.377
19. John Calvin (cited in *Men, Women, and Order in the Church: 3 Sermons*) by Seth Skolnitzky, Presbyterian Heritage Pub; 1992.
20. George Gillespie, *A Treatise of Miscellany Questions, The Works of George Gillespie*, (Still Waters Revival Books, Edmonton, AB; 1846, 1991)
21. Matthew Henry, *Commentary on the Whole Bible, Vol. 6*, (Hendrikson Publishers, Peadbody, MA; 1991), p. 453
22. John Wesley, *Notes on the Bible*, (Francis Asbury Press, Grand Rapids, MI; 1987), p. 517
23. Henry Alford, *Alford's Greek New Testament*, (Guardian Press, Grand Rapids, MI; 1976), p. 563
24. Frederick Godet, Commentary on First Corinthians, (Kregel Publications, Grand Rapids, MI; 1977), p. 54
25. A. R. Fausset, David Brown and Robert Jamieson, *A Commentary, Critical, Experimental, and Practical on the Whole Bible,* 1871, III:II:314
26. M. R. Vincent, *Word Studies in the New Testament,* II:786, 1886
27. G. G. Findlay, *The Expositor's Greek New Testament*, W. Robertson Nicoll, ed., (Eerdmans Publishing Co., Grand Rapids, MI; 1976), II:870-876
28. Joseph Beet, *Joseph Beet's Commentary on St. Paul's Epistles to Corinthians.*
29. C. C. Walker, The Christadelphian. No. 428, Vol. 37, *Let Her Be Covered.*
30. Watchman Nee, *Love One Another*, (reprinted by Christian Fellowship Publishers; Richmond, VA; 1975)
31. A. T. Robertson, *Word Pictures in the New Testament*, (Broadman Press, Nashville, TN; 1931), IV:1 59
32. William Barclay, *The Letters to the Corinthians* Revised Edition, (The Westminster Press, Philadelphia, PA; 1975), p. 97
33. John Murray, *A Letter To The Evangelical Presbyterian Church* (Australia), Presbyteran Reformed Magazine, Winter 1992.
34. James Vernon McGee, *Thru The Bible Commentary Vol. 5*, (Thomas Nelson Publishers, Nashville, TN; 1983), p. 50
35. Charles Ryrie, *The Role of Women in the Church*, (Moody Press, Chicago, IL; 1981, p.74

Let Church History Speak (cont.)

36. Albrect Oepke, Gerhard Kittel, ed., *Theological Dictionary of the New Testament*, (Eerdmans Publishing Co., Grand Rapids, MI; 1965), III:561
37. Bruce K. Waltke, *1 Corinthians 11:2-16: An Interpretation*, (Bibloctheca Sacra 135; 1978), p. 46
38. Ibid., p. 57
39. Noel Weeks, *The Sufficiency of Scripture*, (The Banner of Truth Trust, Edinburgh; 1988), pp. 129-130.
40. Robert D. Culver, *Traditional View – Women in Ministry Four Views*, Bonnidell Clouse and Robert G. Clouse, ed., (InterVarsity Press, Downers Grove, IL; 1989), p. 28
41. John Phillips, *Exploring 1 Corinthians* (Kregel Publications, Grand Rapids, MI; 2002), p. 235
42. M. R. Vincent, *Word Studies in the New Testament*, (MacDonald Publishing Co., McLean VA; 1886)
43. Bruce K. Waltke, op. cit.
44. The Russian Orthodox Cathedral of St. John the Baptist, Washington, D.C., Website: www.stjohndc.org
45. *Parish Life*, Russian Orthodox – October 1991.
46. Ibid.

Who is Paul's Target Audience?

1. John Walvoord, Roy Zuck, David Lowery, *The Bible Knowledge Commentary – 1 Corinthians*, (Victor Books; 1983), p. 505
2. Bruce Terry, *No Such Custom – An Exposition of 1 Corinthians 11:2-16*, (Christian Messenger Publishers, Montezuma Creek, Utah; 1983)
3. Plutarch, *Moralia, The Roman Questions*, 14.
4. *Euripides in Alcest*, ver. 426.
5. Adam Clarke, *Adam Clarke's Commentary on the New Testament*, (http://www.studylight.org/com/acc/view.cgi?book=1co&chapter=011)
6. Plutarch, *The Roman Questions.*
7. M. R. Vincent, op. cit.
8. Cozelmann, *1 Corinthians*, p. 185. Eerdmans, *Concise Bible Handbook*, page 342. Vincent, *Word Studies in the New Testament*, p. 786
9. J. B. Hurley, *Men and Women in Biblical Perspective*, 1981, pp. 254-271
10. Albrecht Oepke, *Theological Dictionary of the New Testament* – "katakalupto," (Eerdmans Publishing)
11. M. R. Vincent, op. cit., II: 786.
12. Albrecht Oepke, op. cit.
13. E. Kasemann, *New Testament Questions of Today*, page 21. Oepke, *Theological Dictionary of the New Testament* Vol. 3, ed. G. Kittel, (Eerdmans; 1965), p. 562.

147

Who is Paul's Target Audience? (cont.)

14. James B. Hurley, *Westminister Theological Journal*, #35 – Winter, 1973
15. Albrecht Oepke, op. cit.
16. John Lightfoot, *A Commentary on the New Testament from the Talmud and Hebraica* (Baker Book House; 1979)
17. William M. Ramsay, *The Cities of St. Paul*, (Baker Book House)
18. David Bercot, op. cit., p. 668
19. David Alexander, Patricia Alexander, *Eerdmans' Handbook to the Bible*, (Lion Publishing; 1973), p. 593
20. Bruce Terry, op. cit.
21. Adam Clarke, op. cit.

Why was Paul Writing?

1. A. R. Fausset, op. cit.

Praise, Ordinances, and the "But"

1. William Moody, *Life of D. L. Moody*, (Fleming H. Revell Co.; 1900), p. 493

What is Headship?

1. G. Morrish, *A Concordance of the Septuagint*, (Zondervan; 1976), p. 136
2. William Morris, *The American Heritage Dictionary*, (Houghton Mifflin Co., Boston; 1979)
3. William MacDonald, *Believer's Bible Commentary*, (Thomas Nelson Publishers, Nashville, TN; 1995), p. 2084
4. J. Hunter, *What The Bible Teaches*, (Ritchie, Scotland; 1982), pp. 124-125
5. J. Allen, *What The Bible Teaches*, (Ritchie, Scotland; 1982), p. 207
6. K. Wuest, *Wuest's Word Studies*, (Eerdmans, Grand Rapids, MI; 1978), Vol. 2, p. 48
7. C. H. Mackintosh, *Short Paper*, Believers Bookshelf, Sunbury, Vol. 2.
8. Matthew Henry, op. cit., 1 Cor. 11

The Glory of Divine Order

1. Plutarch, *Moralia, Sayings of Romans*, Vol. III, translation by Frank Cole Babbitt in the Leob Classical Library edition (Cambridge, Massachusetts: Harvard University Press; 1961), pp. 190-191.
2. *The One Line Bible Thayer's Greek Lexicon*, Woodside Bible Fellowship, Ontario, Canada; Licensed from Institute for Creation Research, 1993.
3. John Calvin (cited in *Men, Women, and Order in the Church*: 3 Sermons by John Calvin), by Seth Skolnitzky, Presbyterian Heritage Pub.
4. Adam Clarke, op. cit.

The Glory of Divine Order (cont.)
5. Albert Barnes, *Barnes Notes* – 1 Cor. 11:6, (Baker Book House, Grand Rapids, MI; reprinted from 1884 edition published by Blackie and Son, London)
6. John Chrysostom, op. cit.
7. John Calvin, op. cit.
8. Harry A. Ironside, *Addresses on The First Epistle To The Corinthians*, (Loizeaux Brothers, Neptune, NJ; 1938), pp. 335-336
9. F. W. Grosheide, *The First Epistle to the Corinthians*, (Eerdmans Publishing, Grand Rapids, MI; 1953), pp. 255-256
10. J. Boyd Nicholson Sr., *The Head Covering – A Biblical Perspective*, (Gospel Folio Press, Grand Rapids, MI)
11. John Calvin, op. cit.
12. David Dickson, *David Dickson's Commentaries on the Epistles* – XI. The Seventh Article Concerning Order and Decency, Printed 1659
13. Warren Wiersbe, *Bible Exposition Commentary* – Vol. 2, Col. 3:18, (Victor Books, Wheaton, IL; 1989), p. 142

Taught by Nature and Unto Angels
1. J. Boyd Nicholson Sr., op. cit.
2. John Lightfoot, op. cit., pp. 236-237
3. Bruce Terry, op. cit.
4. John Calvin, op. cit.
5. Harry A. Ironside, op. cit., pp. 335-336
6. David Dickson, op. cit.
7. J. N. Darby, *Synopsis 1 Corinthians* (Stow Hill Bible and Tract Depot, Kingston, Thames; 1949), p. 175
8. Charles Hodge, *Commentary on the First Epistle to the Corinthians*, (Eerdmans, Grand Rapids, MI; 1976), p. 214
9. Watchman Nee, op. cit.

But When?
1. William MacDonald, op. cit., p. 1785
2. Stephen Hulshizer, *The Truth of Headship and its Symbolic Practices*, (Spread the Word, York, PA; 1992), p. 27
3. Ibid., p. 41
4. R. C. H. Lenski, *Interpretations of I and II Corinthians*, (Wartburg Press, Columbus, Ohio; 1946), pp. 436-437
5. Ibid.

What Constitutes a Head Covering?
1. Dr. Peter J. L. Wee, *Woman's Head Covering & The Glory of God*, (Bethesda Gospel Hall, Singapore)

What Constitutes a Head Covering? (cont.)
2.   David Bercot, op. cit., p. 668
3.   David Bercot, op. cit., p. 690

Arguments and Defense
1.   William MacDonald, op. cit., p. 1786
2.   Dr. H. Wayne House, *The Role of Woman in Ministry Today*, (Thomas Nelson Publishers, Nashville, TN; 1990), p. 121
3.   Dr. N. J. Gourlay, *Church Symbols For Today*, (Walterick Publisher, Kansas City, KS; 1999), p. 171
4.   R. C. H. Lenski, *Interpretations of I and II Corinthians*, pages 439.
5.   R. C. Sproul, *Knowing Scripture*, (Intervarsity Press, Downers Grove, IL; 1977), p. 110
6.   Mary A. Kassian, *Women, Creation and the Fall*, (Crossway Books, Westchester, IL; 1990), p. 1
7.   Ibid., p. 94
8.   Matthew Henry, op. cit., 1 Cor. 11
9.   Dr. John Robbins, *Scripture Twisting in the Seminaries, Part 1: Feminism*, (Trinity Foundation, Jefferson, MD; 1985), p. 26
10. Robert Billings, Jr., *Should Women Speak in the Church Meetings*, (Everyday Publications Inc., Canada; 1993), p. 8
11. Kenneth S. Wuest, *The New Testament: An Expanded Translation* (Eerdmans Publishing Co., Grand Rapids, MI; 1989), 1 Cor. 11:5-6, p. 402

To God Be the Glory
1.   Edythe Draper, *Draper's Quotations from the Christian World* (Tyndale House Publishers Inc., Wheaton, IL – electronic copy)
2.   Matthew Henry, op. cit., Isa. 6
3.   Albert Barnes, op. cit., Isa. 6
4.   William MacDonald, op. cit., p. 944
5.   Warren Wiersbe, *Wiersbe's Expository Outlines on the Old Testament* (Victor Books, Wheaton, IL; 1993), electronic copy
6.   Warren Wiersbe, The Bible Exposition Commentary, Vol. 2 (Victor Books, Wheaton, IL; 1989), p. 582
7.   Enns, P. P., *The Moody Handbook of Theology* (Moody Press, Chicago, IL; 1997, c1989), electronic copy: *Attributes of God* section
8.   Adam Clarke, op. cit., Isa. 6

Conclusion
1.   Dr. Peter J. L. Wee, op. cit.
2.   Watchman Nee, op. cit.

Be Angry and Sin Not

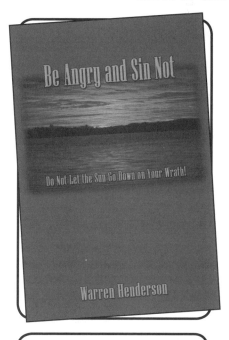

If you mismanage anger, this book will guide you into better self-control. Be Angry And Sin Not tackles such questions as,

* Why am I angry?
* Should I be angry?
* How do I control my angry feelings?
* How can my anger benefit others and serve God?

Binding: Paper

Size: 5.5" X 8.0"

Page Count: 122 pages

Item #: B-7051

ISBN : 1897117051

Genre: Devotional/ Christian Living

Warren Henderson
Once an aerospace engineer, now serves the Lord with his wife Brenda in "full time" ministry. They are commended by Believers Bible Chapel in Rockford, Illinois. Warren is an itinerant Bible teacher and is involved in writing, evangelism, church planting and foreign missionary work.

GOSPEL FOLIO PRESS
I WILL PUBLISH THE NAME OF THE LORD

304 Killaly St. West | Port Colborne | ON | L3K 6A6 | Canada | 1 800 952 2382 | E-mail: info@gospelfolio.com | www.gospelfolio.com

BEHOLD THE SAVIOUR

CONTEMPLATING THE VAST WORTH OF THE SAVIOUR

It was refreshing and encouraging to read a book, that did not focus on man's needs or a "how to" method for success. *Behold the Saviour* focuses on the Lord Jesus: His Godhood, human goodness and glories as revealed in the multi-faceted presentation of Holy Scriptures. For when we behold Him in His glory we are *"changed into the same image from glory to glory, even as by the Spirit of the Lord"* (2 Cor. 3:18).

—Anonymous Pre-Publication Reviewer (to Christ be the glory!)

Charles Haddon Spurgeon once said, "The more you know about Christ, the less you will be satisfied with superficial views of Him." The more we know of Christ, the more we will love and experience Him. This study has refreshed my soul. In the long hours of contemplating the vast worth that the Father attaches to every aspect of the Saviour's life, I have been encouraged to love Him more. If you're feeling a bit dry or spiritually despondent, *Behold the Saviour* afresh – and may the Holy Spirit ignite your passion for Christ and invigorate your ministry for Him.   —Warren Henderson

---

Binding: **Paper**

Size: **5.5" X 8.5"**

Page Count: **208 pages**

Item #: **B-7272**

ISBN : **1-897117-27-2**

Genre: **Devotional**

Warren Henderson
An aerospace engineer, who now serves the Lord with his wife Brenda in "full time" ministry. They are recommended by Believers Bible Chapel in Rockford, Illinois. Warren is an itinerant Bible teacher and is involved in writing, evangelism, and church planting.

GOSPEL FOLIO PRESS
I WILL PUBLISH THE NAME OF THE LORD

304 Killaly St. West | Port Colborne | ON | L3K 6A6 | Canada | 1 800 952 2382 | E-mail: info@gospelfolio.com | www.gospelfolio.com

The Fruitful Vine

A CELEBRATION OF BIBLICAL WOMANHOOD

The Fruitful Vine contains six sections. The first, The Marital Union, supplies the biblical foundation for the remainder of the book: Why was marriage instituted, and what was God's best plan for marriage? The chapter "To Marry or Not?" offers guidance and encouragement to unmarried women, both those called to "singleness" and those "maids in waiting." The following three sections pertain to the natural roles a married woman will find the most joy in fulfilling - namely, being a companion to her husband, bearing and nurturing children, and keeping an ordered home. The fifth section, The Autumn Years, provides counsel to the "empty-nesters" and encouragement for widows. The final section provides a character sketch of a spiritually-minded woman and the types of ministry she may engage in. Through Scripture, God has revealed both what He finds beautiful in a woman and what He expects of her.

Binding: **Paper**
Size: **5.5" X 8.0"**
Page Count: **172 pages**
Item #: **B-7132**
ISBN : **1-897117-13-2**
Genre: **Devotional**

Warren Henderson
An aerospace engineer, who now serves the Lord with his wife Brenda in "full time" ministry. They are commended by Believers Bible Chapel in Rockford, Illinois. Warren is an itinerant Bible teacher and is involved in writing, evangelism, and church planting.

GOSPEL FOLIO PRESS
I WILL PUBLISH THE NAME OF THE LORD

304 Killaly St. West | Port Colborne | ON | L3K 6A6 | Canada | 1 800 952 2382 | E-mail: info@gospelfolio.com | www.gospelfolio.com

The Olive Plants
Raising Spiritual Children

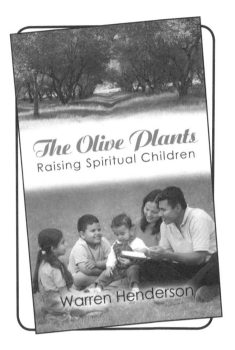

Most of the Christian children's ministry today is aimed at raising "moral" children. The teaching of right and wrong is necessary, but this agenda will fall pitifully short of producing "spiritual" children. Children must develop morally, physically, spiritually, emotionally, and academically, to really thrive and reach God's full potential for their lives. When children have a balanced development they lay hold of self-acceptance and self-awareness of their calling in God's master plan. In so doing, they gain a sense of importance and security—God is in control and has a plan for my life.

Binding: **Paper**

Size: **5.5" X 8.5"**

Page Count: **238 pages**

Item #: **B-7514**

ISBN : **978-1897117-51-4**

Genre: **Christian Living**

Warren Henderson

An aerospace engineer, he now serves the Lord with his wife Brenda in "full time" ministry. They are commended by Believers Bible Chapel in Rockford, Illinois. Warren is an itinerant Bible teacher and is involved in writing, evangelism, and church planting. He is the author of Be Angry and Sin Not, Behold the Saviour, The Fruitful Vine, Glories Seen and Unseen, Hallowed Be Thy Name, Mind Frames, Seeds of Destiny, and Your Home: A Birthing Place for Heaven.

GOSPEL FOLIO PRESS
I WILL PUBLISH THE NAME OF THE LORD

304 Killaly St. West | Port Colborne | ON | L3K 6A6 | Canada | 1 800 952 2382 | E-mail: info@gospelfolio.com | www.gospelfolio.com

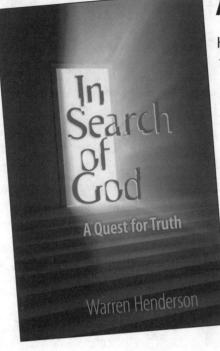